The 7 Step eBook

"I read the first copy of The 7 Step eBook and found it to be a comprehensive source of practical information to create, market and publish eBooks."

Alan Yong, CEO, Times Telecom Inc.

"I had the opportunity to be the first author to test 'The 7 Step eBook' to publish my book "Stories from Things." After my experience with traditional publishers, I am excited as I now have the ability to publish my books, keep my rights and a bigger portion of the sales income."

Sultan Somjee, PhD, Author

"I am a freelance editor, but that didn't prepare me to assist in the publishing end of an eBook. Trying to maneuver my way through all the instructions for preparing, publishing and marketing, was a real challenge. I really do wish I had a copy of this book when I was first getting my husband's book online. It would have saved me a lot of grief."

Frankie Sutton, Editor

The 7 Step eBook

How to Publish and Sell eBooks

SADIQ SOMJEE

Published by GeoEdge Consulting Ltd.

Vancouver, Canada.

The 7 Step eBook

First Edition 2011

http://www.the7stepeBook.com/

Amazon Kindle ISBN: 978-0-9869273-0-0
EPUB eBook ISBN: 978-0-9869273-2-4

Print Book ISBN-13: 978-1466212879
Print Book ISBN-10: 146621287X

DEDICATION

To authors, artists, poets and retailers for democratizing the new online publishing industry.

I wish you success.

CONTENTS

ACKNOWLEDGMENTS

With thanks to

My wife Farida

My son Zia for the cover design

Author Sultan Somjee for testing the 7 Steps

http://storiesfromthings.blogspot.com

Frankie Sutton for editorial assistance

fjstton@yahoo.com

Artist Nadia Fay

http://nadiafay.blogspot.com

INTRODUCTION

The eBook market has exploded and eBook sales have surpassed both hard and soft cover book sales according to Jeff Bezos, founder and CEO of Amazon (Amazon news release, May 19, 2011.) Yet the eBook market is still in its infancy. It's now the time to ride the online publishing wave as an author. The confluence of tablet computers, eReaders, mobile phones, the internet, electronic miniaturization, storage technology, and wireless technology is further fueling this growth. Social networking and online tools such as Facebook, Twitter, Google+, WordPress, Blogger, Amazon and Apple iBooks have become the new platforms to sell your work. The internet has opened a broad landscape of tools and technologies to publish and market your work. All these technologies can work in harmony for you and are yours to orchestrate.

The technology is surprisingly simple to apply once you see how it is done. This book will show you how to publish an eBook, use a blog and social networking to stand out in this noisy internet space. It will leave you with a working framework and a strategy that you can grow with and customize for your niche market.

New disruptive technologies are challenging the publishing industry. The good news is that all the online publishers want to publish your work because it is the author's content that sells eReader devices (such as the Kindle, iPad, Nook, Kobo and Sony.)

These eReader devices connect directly to online bookstores, which in turn sell eBooks. Online bookstores on Amazon, Apple, Barnes & Noble, Google, Sony and Chapters work hard to attract buyers and sell books. Self-publishers in turn can use online bookstores to promote and sell their eBooks. By publishing your books to online bookstores, your book gains visibility on search engines such as Google, Yahoo and Bing.

Phenomenal eBook growth

There has been phenomenal growth in eReaders. The Amazon Kindle, Apple iPad, Sony, Chapters Kobo, Blackberry PlayBook, and the Barnes & Noble Nook have become common consumer items. The Samsung Galaxy and Motorola XOOM run on Google's Android platform and others such as Dell and HTC devices run on Microsoft's mobile platform. The proliferation of these devices has opened up a huge market for eBooks. The dropping cost and mainstream use is great news for the author, as these devices are additional platforms to sell eBooks.

Not including the global population, USA and Canada have a combined population of 344 million people. As of this writing there were over a 100 million iPhones, 25 million iPads, millions of Kindles, Nooks, Sony's and other devices. In addition, eBook reading applications are available on a number of other mobile devices, which further expand the eBook market. For example, Amazon also publishes Kindle reader applications for the iPad, PC, Mac and Android devices. If you do the math on selling a $2.99 eBook with a 70% return to 0.1% (or 344,000) of the

North American population, it works out to be over $700,000 back to the author. This is not easy to achieve, however, a few indie authors have indeed sold over million eBooks. This book will explore some of the strategies these indie authors used.

Malcolm Gladwell writes about this kind of viral growth phenomenon in his book "The Tipping Point." Gladwell talks about this contagious consumer behavior. Like cell phones, eReader devices have reached a tipping point where everybody wants an eReader device like a Kindle or an iPad. It is contagious and growing virally across all age groups. In turn, the sales of these gadgets increase the demand for eBooks and vice versa.

Online storefronts, such as the Amazon Kindle bookstore, Apple iBooks and others, are creating service portals for buyers known as cloud services. They make money by attracting buyers to their online portals. Companies such as Sony, Blackberry, Apple, Nokia, Microsoft, Samsung and many others are jumping into the consumer gadget and platform wars because they see the long-term demand. These devices feed the demand, the service portals cater to the demand and the authors create content for this viral eBook trend. This is good news for the independent authors and publishers.

Evidence of eBook publishing success

Self-publishing is now mainstream and a respectable way to publish. Many successful authors got their start this way. For example, Amanda Hocking gave up on her attempts to find a traditional publisher and self-published. She sold at least a million eBooks priced from 99 cents and up. By self-publishing, Hocking built a name, a readership, and got the attention of the publishers. It gave her the leverage to attract and negotiate a better deal with a traditional publisher. Indie authors such as J.A Konrath and John Locke have also occupied spots on the Amazon top 100.

An Amazon news release (SEATTLE, Jan 12, 2011) stated that the first author to surpass the one million mark on the Kindle was Stieg Larsson, of the Millennium Trilogy. James Patterson who writes a number of genres was the second author to pass the one million Kindle sales mark. More recently, Nora Roberts passed the one million Kindle sales mark. All these established authors had access to the online market as you do today. In fact, according to a recent Amazon press release, John Locke became the first Indie author to join the "Kindle Million Club." Soon after the press release, John Locke signed on with publisher Simon & Schuster. One can only speculate on the deal he negotiated after selling over a million books as an indie. These indie authors have published multiple books and have used eBooks to build their readership using online promotional tools and pricing strategies.

Traditional publishers caught off guard

Traditional publishers (Figure 1) continue to hold onto their classic model. Initially, the new author makes a pitch and then submits a proposal for review. If successful, a manuscript is submitted and a contract may be signed. The new author may get a royalty of 10% for printed book to 25% for an eBook, of which the agent typically takes 15%. Publishers may take months to review the book, and often take 18 to 24 months before the book is published. Next, distributers are engaged to ship print books to brick-and-mortar bookstores, where the book is required to prove itself through sales within a few weeks, or else is removed from the valuable inventory space. Publishers may hold back the author's commission to cover the cost of returns.

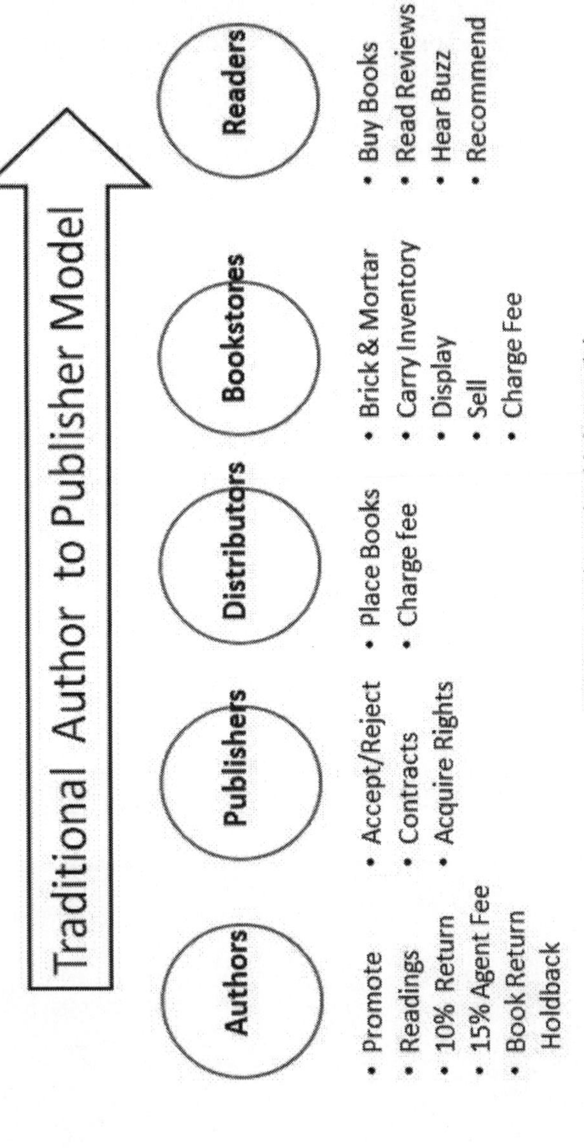

Figure 1 – Traditional Publisher Model

In the new model (Figure 2), eBooks are published online by authors and may be purchased from a number of easy to access online bookstores such as the Amazon Kindle store, Apple iBooks store and the Barnes & Noble Nook store. The new publishers also distribute, sell and deliver the books to the readers online. This model cuts out the traditional publisher, the agent, the distributor, and the bookstore, which reduces the overall cost to the reader. In addition, eBooks do not require printing, packaging, shipping and distribution thus eliminating these costs. Amazon which has the largest eBook market share offers a 70% royalty option for books priced from $2.99 to $9.99. Best of all, the indie author can set the retail price and retain all digital, print and movie rights.

Print books can be set up with print on demand (POD) companies such as Lighting Source and CreateSpace. There is no book inventory required and no significant cost. The author sets the book price and the POD house fulfills the order by printing and shipping the book to the customer. POD companies also provide services such as adding your book to their distribution channels.

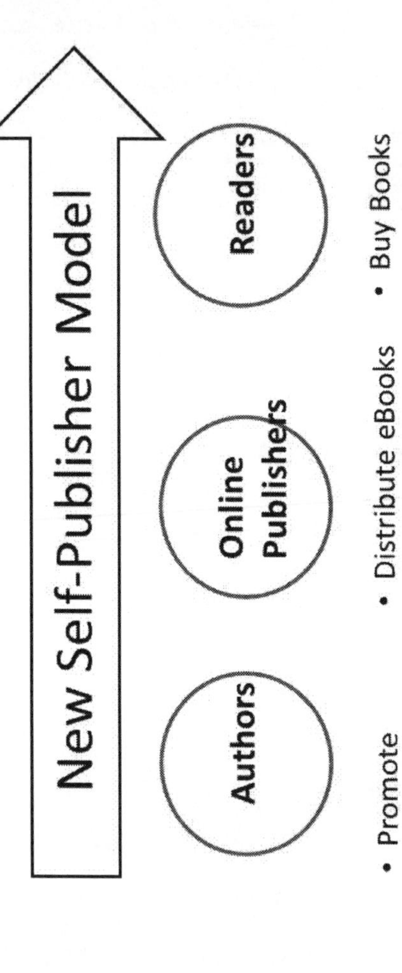

Figure 2 – Self Publisher Model

With wireless technology, online stores, eReaders and the internet, the distribution of eBooks is instant. According to Mark Coker, the founder of Smashwords, some indie authors are outselling print books a 1,000 to 1 (source: Bay Area Independent Publishers Association – May 14, 2011.)

Amazon has changed the game with the low cost Kindle and online eBook sales. Apple iPad with iBooks is also a major player as are Sony, Chapters, Google and Barnes & Noble. With the new web-publishing model, authors are steadily moving to self-publishing.

Authors now have the tools to not only convert their books into eBooks but also access global markets by leveraging online bookstores, search engines and social networking.

Authors left unprepared

Although authors have produced great material, they find the online world of publishing, branding, marketing and selling complex, if not intimidating. This is not surprising as the internet has a lot of disjointed, confusing and often contradictory information.

My purpose in writing this book is to present online publishing information in a simple, concise and comprehensive way to non-technical authors. Having researched eBook publishing for six months, I began writing and simultaneously testing the readability of each chapter with an author.

The confluence of technology has leveled the playing field between the traditional publishers and independent authors. This technology is available, easy and accessible to any author who wants to self-publish.

Empowering the author

This book will show you how to create an effective marketing and publishing framework for your book in 7 simple steps. You will learn how to publish your book to an eBook and a print book, connect on social media, and create a blog free. It will also describe how these technologies work together to help you customize your online brand and attract the right customers. You will learn how to improve your visibility and execute strategies to turn online book browsers into buyers.

The online tools will open up a huge market for your eBook. It is a win-win proposal because everyone gets a cut of the sale of your book. Online distributers like Amazon and Apple iBooks provide a service by allowing buyers to download a sample and buy your eBook. They share the revenue and the author gets access to a massive market and distribution channel. The cut the author makes is much higher (35% to 70%) than the traditional publisher model (10% to 25%). In the new online sales model, the author's marketing efforts translate into direct revenue. The selling, pricing, distribution and money collection is in your control. All you need to do is publish and promote effectively using existing online communities, tools, partners and affiliates.

Book approach

I was fortunate to find an author who was not technical and wanted to have his work published and sold online. This prototyping approach tested the publishing framework presented in this book. In the process of testing, the technical language was simplified for the non-technical author.

How will this book benefit you?

On completion, you will have the knowledge to build a working framework to market, sell and publish your books.

The eBook market has clearly exploded and it is on the rise with the confluence of eReaders, mobile devices and online services. Knowing how to exploit this new online publishing model is essential for today's author.

THE FUNDAMENTALS

This chapter is designed to provide readers of all levels enough knowledge to proceed with the rest of this book.

Many authors have heard of popular social networking sites such as Facebook and Twitter. Some already use these tools, though not all use them effectively. Some do not know where to start or how to make these tools work for them. We will start with the basics and then build on how to make these online tools work for you.

What is an eBook?

An eBook is short for "electronic book"; eBooks can be read on eBook reading devices known as eReaders. eBooks are basically digital books. When publishers ask for your book's digital rights, you are essentially giving them your eBook rights. The most popular eReader is the Amazon's Kindle. Other popular eReaders include the iPad, Sony, Barnes & Noble's Nook and devices running the Google Android operating system.

eReaders are light and small which make them easy to carry while travelling and as bedside readers. The owners of these devices cover a large demographic consisting of seniors, professionals and youth. eReaders can store thousands of books ranging from children's books, fiction, how-to books, graphic novels and reference books. Are you thinking about where your book fits in this demographic?

Once an eBook is purchased, it can be downloaded instantly via wireless. Vendors such as Amazon and Apple keep your eBook purchase history and back-up your books online, so your eBooks can be accessed in case you break or upgrade your eReader.

eBooks can be bookmarked and the reader can go back to where he or she left off. The table of contents is typically hyperlinked so the reader can jump to any location by simply clicking on the link. eBook users can increase the size of the font, making it popular for the visually impaired and older readers. In addition, the audio feature allows the eBooks to be read aloud. Many features such as highlighting text, searching for words, and adding notes are available today and more features are constantly being added to new models. The more expensive iPad has color and is interactive making it popular for children's books and games. All these features are designed to enhance the reader's experience.

What is a blog and why an author needs one?

A blog at its simplest level is basically your website on the internet. Authoring and maintaining a blog is called blogging. A blogger is a person who posts articles and pictures on a blog. It is a free self-publishing platform to share your thoughts and articles. There are many types of blogs spanning a number of subject areas such as art, poetry, cooking, gardening, and book reviews.

Your blog is a public portal, where your customers can come to read your posts, find out more about you, your book, and where to purchase it. It is free alternative to having and maintaining a website. You do need any specialized technical knowledge to set up a blog. Google's Blogger takes a few clicks to set up and you do not have to worry about domains, hosting or fees of any kind. Having a blog for your book is an essential sales and marketing tool.

What is Facebook and why use it?

Facebook is a social networking website, which is used to connect with friends, customers and fans. An increasing number of authors are using Facebook to connect to and attract readers. Facebook authors can create an author profile page and share information publicly. Along with your blog and Twitter, Facebook with over 750 million users is an important component of your online sales and marketing toolbox.

What is Twitter and why tweet?

Twitter is a social networking tool. Twitter is a service that allows users to send short text messages or tweets out to the internet. People set up Twitter accounts to say things and voice opinions on wide range of topics that vary from personal tweets, technology, finance, books and so on.

If used well, Twitter is a powerful marketing tool for the indie publisher. Twitter, like Facebook is also a great way to keep on top of subjects you want to follow. Twitter lets you connect with reviewers, authors, readers, magazines, and other players.

As of this writing Twitter had 200 million users who send out a billion tweets a week. This is not a market you want to ignore. People can send and receive messages (tweets) to and from the public or just their followers. Tweets are publicly visible by default. However users can restrict messages to just their followers if they elect to do so. For authors, public visibility is a good thing, as you want to gain maximum market exposure. Twitter is a serious mainstream marketing tool and not just something that teenagers use to chatter with. Search engines giving your book global exposure will find your tweets on book announcements and reader comments.

What is SEO?

SEO stands for Search Engine Optimization. SEO is essentially things you can do that will get more visitors to land on your website or blog. When someone on the planet does a web search for a keyword and he or she is a potential buyer of your book, you want that person to come to your site. SEO makes you visible on search engines like Google and Yahoo. The benefit of applying SEO is that your book and blog posts will be easier to find on the internet. Step 2 will show you how to leverage keywords to attract the right customers to your blog and book retailer sites.

The eBook success triangle

Figure 3, basically shows to be successful, first start with a great quality book, next build a well thought out marketing plan, follow up with a blog that will attract the right customers, publish your eBook and connect with your readers using Twitter, Facebook and other social media tools.

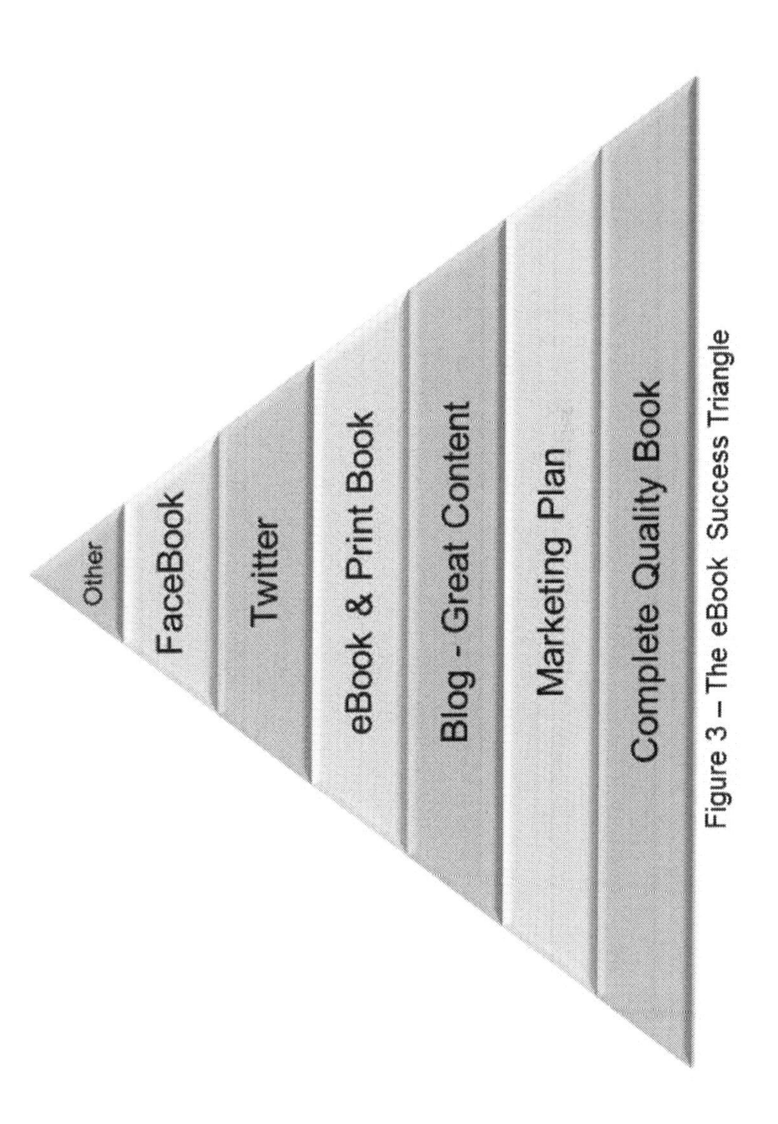

Figure 3 – The eBook Success Triangle

The order of importance of the success triangle starts from the base and ends at the tip. After all the Egyptians built the foundation first, as you must with a quality book.

The marketing plan will be your guiding compass that you will keep coming back to and enhancing as you learn more about your readers (Step 2.)

Based on your marketing plan, start building your online presence beginning with a blog. The blog needs to be engaging and a showcase of your skills as an author. It needs to attract the right customers by design (Step 3.)

Step 4 will show you how to format and publish an eBook and a print on demand book to major retailers such Amazon, Apple and Barnes & Noble.

Once you have built this foundation, Steps 3 and 5 will show you how to generate interest in your work and interact online with Twitter and Facebook. Perhaps you are one of the 750 million people connected to friends and family via Facebook, you may even have a blog and a Twitter account. Sending out random tweets or Facebook updates will not add much without a well-planned and orchestrated marketing plan (Steps 2 to 7.)

At the tip of the triangle, "other" includes websites, social bookmarking sites, video promotion and online advertising (Step 7.)

Whether you are writing fiction or non-fiction books the 7 steps will demonstrate how to get maximum exposure.

Social media, internet and eBook players

Companies have built privileged access to millions of customers and they want to grow their market share by connecting you to your readers. These companies in turn collect and use this valuable marketing information to grow and make decisions. Some of the key players in this space are:

- Google Blogger, WordPress, and Yahoo360 blog applications.
- Facebook, Twitter, LinkedIn, Google+ and MySpace social networking sites.
- Amazon, Apple, Sony, Google, Chapters/Indigo, and Barnes & Noble and Smashwords online bookstores.
- iPad, Kindle, Sony, Kobo, PlayBook, Galaxy, Nook and Android tablets, mobiles and eReaders.

- Lighting source, CreateSpace, Blurb and Lulu, and other print on demand services (POD).
- Google, Yahoo, Bing, Ask and AOL search engines
- YouTube, Vimeo, SlideShare and podcast video sites
- Digg, StumbleUpon, Reddit and Delicious social bookmarking sites.

This book will show you how all these sites can work together for you and which ones you really need to use. The approach will be selecting a few to keep it simple and minimize your effort to 4 hours a week, once you have built your platform in step 3.

Online privacy

What you say on the web remains on the web, so use these tools professionally. Your tweets, Facebook updates, comments on other sites, and your blog posts are all public. Facebook is your public profile; many people keep a private Facebook profile for friends and family, and a public one for their product, service or business. A Facebook author page is a good way to separate your private network from your public profile. Having an author page does not restrict you from sending updates to your private network.

The real power of these tools comes from the access to broad markets, so to market your work you need to use social networking. Some writers use a pen name, which may be carried over to social media. In most cases as an author, you are a brand known for a certain genre and you are what you share online.

Publishing an eBook

Like a print copy, an eBook may be self-published or published by your publisher. An eBook is just another medium to publish your book. Just because your work is on an eBook, it does not mean it is self-published. Traditional publishers typically keep the eBook digital rights in addition to print rights.

In order to self-publish your work to an eBook, you need to modify your book into a format that will be accepted by the distributer. For example, if your book is in Microsoft Word format, it will need to be modified so it can be published to an eBook since each eBook vendor has different formatting requirements. Publishing your work to these multiple formats will be discussed in Step 4.

As an indie author, you can publish your book to an eBook as well as print book. Have your book in both mediums as both have large customer bases. One medium is no more prestigious than the other is. eBooks typically have a lower price point than print books and are instantly available to the customer's eReader. With instant gratification, customers are more likely to impulse buy eBooks. This availability works well with online marketing strategies discussed in Step 2. eBooks also give you name recognition by listing your book on well-established retail sites, which in turn translate to sales for both print and eBooks.

How many pages should I write?

The pages for an eBook vary widely. Aim for quality and try to give the readers maximum value and more for their money. A novella or short novel according to Wikipedia is anywhere from 10,000 to 70,000 words. For a first novel, most publishers want 80,000 to 120,000 words. Reference books could be 8,000 to 12,000 words or about 30 to 50 pages. There are no hard and fast rules for eBooks.

The number of pages determines price, it is unreasonable to sell a 10-page book for $15. Ensure your book has valuable content or a good story to establish your name as an author. eBooks can be priced anywhere from free to $9.99 and up. Your price point will depend on how similar books are priced, what your customers are willing to pay, and the demand for your book.

Quality and design

On the question book quality, the eBooks lack formal regulation. Reviewers on the internet will decide if the book is any good, Quality books will float to the top and the ones with just the hype will sink into obscurity. Traditional publishers controlled formal regulation as only they had access to the distribution channels and bookstores. Now that authors have direct access to readers via online retailers such as Amazon, the free market will decide if the book is worthy.

It is important to have your book edited, there are many reasonably priced editors available online such as Frankie Sutton mentioned in the acknowledgment. Although I had used friends and family as proofreaders, Frankie Sutton helped me clean up my book. Nothing derails a book quicker than misspellings and grammar issues.

There have been a lot of spam books that online retailers are now beginning to catch. These poor quality books are giving eBooks a bad name. To be established as a credible author requires attention to quality.

A great cover design with a catchy book title and quality content are all just as important for an eBook as they are for a print book. Your eBook has to stand out from the crowd.

Life of an eBook

Online storage and disk space is relatively inexpensive and your book will be around for a long time. Keep your master copy backed up and updated periodically to the latest version of Microsoft Word, WordPerfect, or any other word processor you use. In the unlikely event that your material disappears online, you can always republish.

eReader devices

The big three eReader devices are Amazon's Kindle, Apple's iPad and Barnes & Noble's Nook. All have websites (portals) for eBooks, with Amazon being number one so far. The other significant players are Google Android, Sony and Chapters/Indigo Kobo devices.

If you want a simple low cost eReader that just reads books, the Kindle is for you. If you like to play games, watch movies, listen to music and read books the iPad, Android and Windows based tablets are for you. It's all about personal preference and it's about access to books and price. Amazon, Apple, Barnes & Noble, and Chapters/Indigo all sell books online.

Vendors earn by selling eBooks on proprietary devices, but they also make money by selling eBooks on other devices. For example, Amazon has developed Kindle reader applications for the iPad, Android, Mac, Windows and other platforms. With the Kindle reader application, these devices can be used to purchase Kindle eBooks directly from Amazon in a few clicks.

eBook communities and resources

Many writers have asked if there are support communities for eBooks. Some great online communities on Amazon and Smashwords are available for authors. They provide support and a service to convert your eBooks into multiple online formats. Smashwords connects independent resources that provide cover design, eBook format conversion and material on their site to support eBook publishing. Smashwords also distributes your eBooks to major eBook retailers.

Online communities such as Goodreads, CreateSpace, Smashwords, Amazon publishing forums and Yahoo groups are good sources for support and information on eBook publishing, marketing and collaboration. You can connect with readers and authors to discuss everything books on these sites. Other blogs and communities you choose to participate in and connect with are all sources of exposure and information.

Earlier this year, I attended the annual Self-publishers Online Conference (SPOC) put on by Logical Expressions. The affordable conference is well worth the money. The topics ranged from book cover design, online marketing, developing your book title and many other sessions from established authors. I would recommend this conference for authors who want to self-publish.

http://www.selfpublishersonlineconference.com

eBook piracy

In the past online piracy has been a major problem for the music and movie business. With the rise of eBook sales, piracy is now a problem for eBooks. Printed books can also be scanned, digitized and put on the web by piracy organizations. For example, every Harry Potter title is available from pirate sites even though J. K. Rowling refused to make the Harry Potter books available digitally (before the "Pottermore" announcement.) Not publishing digitally does not stop piracy, especially if your book is popular.

Protection from Digital Rights Management (DRM) was not effective in the music industry and there is no indication it will prevent eBooks from being copied. DRM is not effective and is often a nuisance to legitimate customers as it prevents them from using the books the way they want. Software programmers who have the inclination and time can break DRM code or could download software to remove DRM. This is too much trouble for most people, as they would rather pay the $1.99 or $7.99 for an eBook that downloads to their eReader right away. Piracy will no doubt occur in a small segment of the population and little can be done about it, other than pricing your book reasonably and distributing it widely to all popular eReaders. In other words, wide distribution and availability will help lessen the impact of piracy.

The enforcement of global piracy is weak as it is difficult to chase and shut down illegal pirate sites. The bottom line is that people who own eReader devices such as the Kindle are unlikely to bother with pirated books.

Contracts and payments

Before you publish your book as an eBook with a retailer such as Amazon, you will create an account and enter into a contract with respect to royalties, sales reporting and payment schedules. These next generation retailers take care of the order fulfillment for you; they take the eBook order, deliver it to the customers' device and deposit a payment to your account on an agreed schedule. They also provide monthly or periodic reports so you can track your sales and revenue.

You do not need to invest any money to publish an eBook, the online retailer takes a cut of the sales and then you get back a royalty. As an indie author, you maintain all the rights, you can pull your book out of circulation, update your book and price it as you please.

Does an eBook need an ISBN number?

An ISBN (International Standard Book Number) is a number that uniquely identifies each specific edition of a book or book-like product. You do not need an ISBN if you publish your book electronically on the Amazon Kindle. Online retailers such as Apple and Barnes & Noble require one. Many online services will provide one for a fee. CreateSpace provides free ISBN numbers for your print book and Smashwords will provide one for your eBook.

If you intend to sell books in physical bookstores, educational institutions, or to libraries, I would recommend getting an ISBN number. This will give you more exposure and channels to sell your books.

In the USA **bowker.com** is a service that provides ISBN number to authors and publishers for a fee.

In Canada, you can get one free from:

www.collectionscanada.gc.ca/publishers

Copyright

Copyright registration is voluntary; it protects original works of authorship. Registration is recommended because a public record and certificate of registration may be eligible for damages in successful litigation. Registration is accepted as evidence in a court of law.

At the very minimum, include a copyright in your book. It is a good idea to register your copyright for a small fee.

In the USA, you can register your copyright at:

http://www.copyright.gov

In Canada, copyrights can be registered at:

http://www.cb-cda.gc.ca

STEP 1: CONCEPTS & ORGANIZATION

Figure 4 on the next page outlines the 7 steps required to build your platform. Each step may take from a few hours to a few days depending on your knowledge and time. Complete each step at your own pace or read through the 7 Steps as you work on your book.

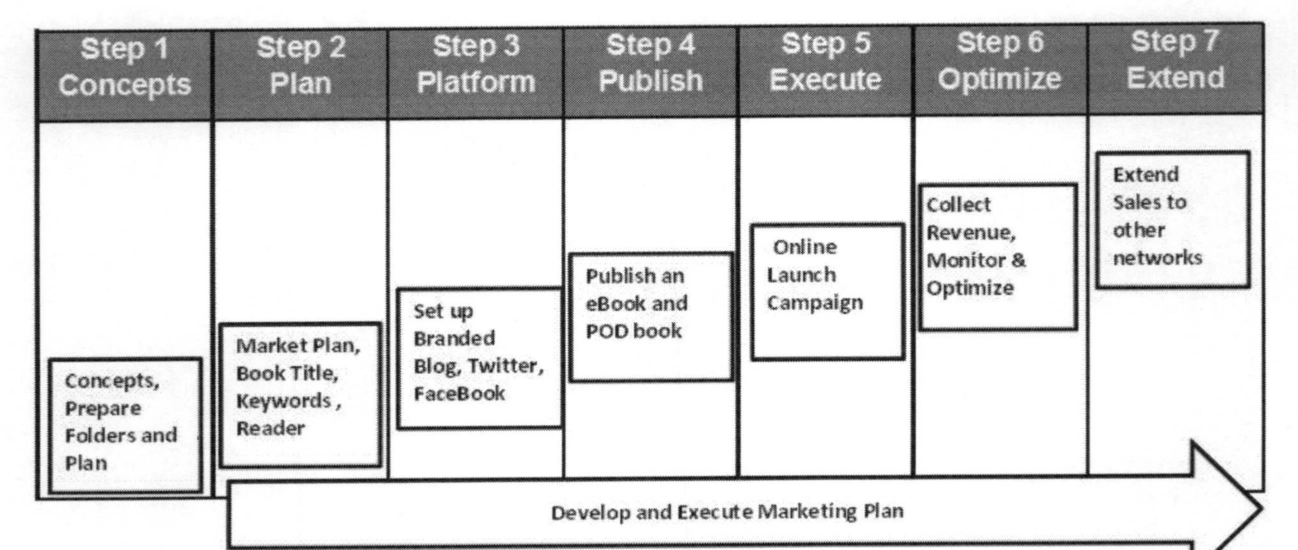

Figure 4: The 7 Steps

Step 1, gives you an overview of how online marketing works and describes a file and folder system to help keep your material organized.

In Step 2, a marketing plan is developed around your reader profile. Once you understand your reader profile and develop a marketing plan, the rest of the steps are mechanical. Step 2 is the strategy behind your online sales platform.

In Step 3, you will build your online platform with social media and blogs.

Using a simple system in Step 4, you will have the knowledge to publish your book to various eBook formats such as the Kindle, Nook, iPad, Sony and others. The keywords, book title and description developed in Step 2 will be put into play in Steps 3 and 4, where you publish and customize your book pages on retail websites.

Step 5 is the execution of your marketing campaign using your online sales platform. The completion of Step 5 is a major milestone because at this stage you will have published your book, launched your campaign, and will be all set to collect revenue from both your eBook and pBook sales.

In Step 6, you will be introduced to tools to monitor what your readers are interested in and keep tabs on how many visitors land on your site. These tools will provide you the information to adjust your campaign and focus on blog posts that resonate with your customers.

In Step 7, you will extend your reach by leveraging other social media like videos, slides, podcasts and social bookmarking.

How it works – from reader to bank

I was sitting at a coffee shop with an author, explaining how social media, search engines and eBook retailers such as Amazon work for the self-published author. I sketched out Figure 5 on the back of a paper napkin for this aspiring author. Eventually, this sketch and conversation ended up becoming the heart of the book.

How do search engines, Facebook, Twitter and your Blog work together to help you market, sell and collect revenue from your eBook? Figure 5 shows the sea of potential readers on the internet using search keywords to find topics of interest to them.

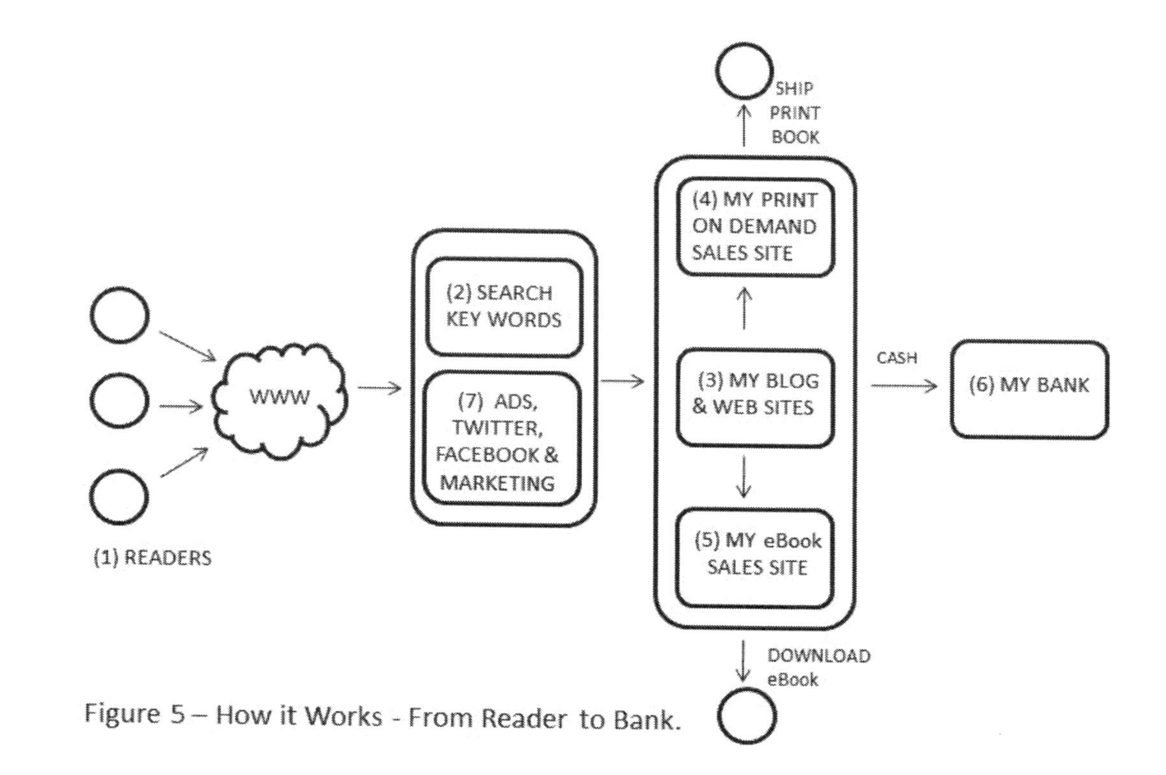

Figure 5 – How it Works - From Reader to Bank.

It is important to understand how blogs, social media and book sales all work together in harmony. Each of these online tools feeds on the other; it is a symbiotic relationship. A tweet will drive visitors to your blog; your blog will direct customers to purchase your eBook.

Your job is to get buyers to land on your blog or to your eBook retail sites. Once a visitor has landed on your site, you need to convince the visitor to buy your eBook. The converted customer then purchases the book from your online booksellers and the money magically appears in your bank account.

Follow Figure 5 and see how the money flows from readers to your bank account:

(1) Readers (circles) are fishing for information on the internet (WWW) using search engines such as Google, Yahoo and Bing.

(2) Using the right combination of search keywords on your blog and book sales site, you want to hook customers to land on your eBook, print book and blog, web, retail sites (3, 4, and 5.)

(3) Once the customer has landed on your blog, you need to convince them that your book is worth buying and direct them to the eBook retailer or print on demand site (POD.)

(4) Customers arrive to the POD sales site either directly from the internet or from your blog site to purchase a print copy. In this book, we will set up the print book using CreateSpace and sell on Amazon.com.

(5) Customers arrive to your eBook sales site, either directly from the internet, or from your blog site to make a purchase. eBook retailers include Apple, Amazon, Barnes & Noble, and Chapters.

(6) When a sale is made, the customer downloads the eBook onto an eReader and your eBook retailers deposit money to your bank account.

(7) Targeted ads, tweets and Facebook posts get more readers to visit your blog, eBook and pBook retail sites (3, 4, and 5.)

Note: Customers may also arrive directly from the internet to your sales sites, based on keywords set up on your retail sites. Setting up the right keywords or tags on your author page on Amazon, Smashwords and Apple iBooks is a key strategy in Step 4 when you publish your eBook. Amazon, Apple, Barnes & Noble, Google, Chapters and Sony are some of the places where customers may buy your book. The keywords you develop in Step 2 will be critical to attracting your readers to these online retail sites. These established retailers have mature and well-designed search engines to help customers locate the right books. Millions of eyeballs scan these retail sites daily, so spend all the time you need developing your market plan in Step 2. In addition, guest blogging, YouTube videos and being active on other blogs will attract readers to your sites.

Organize your folders

Set up your basic folders to help keep your files organized. Use the folder structure shown in Figure 6, for each book you have.

Create a basic administration (admin) folder to keep important emails, copyright, permissions to use material, contract and other information.

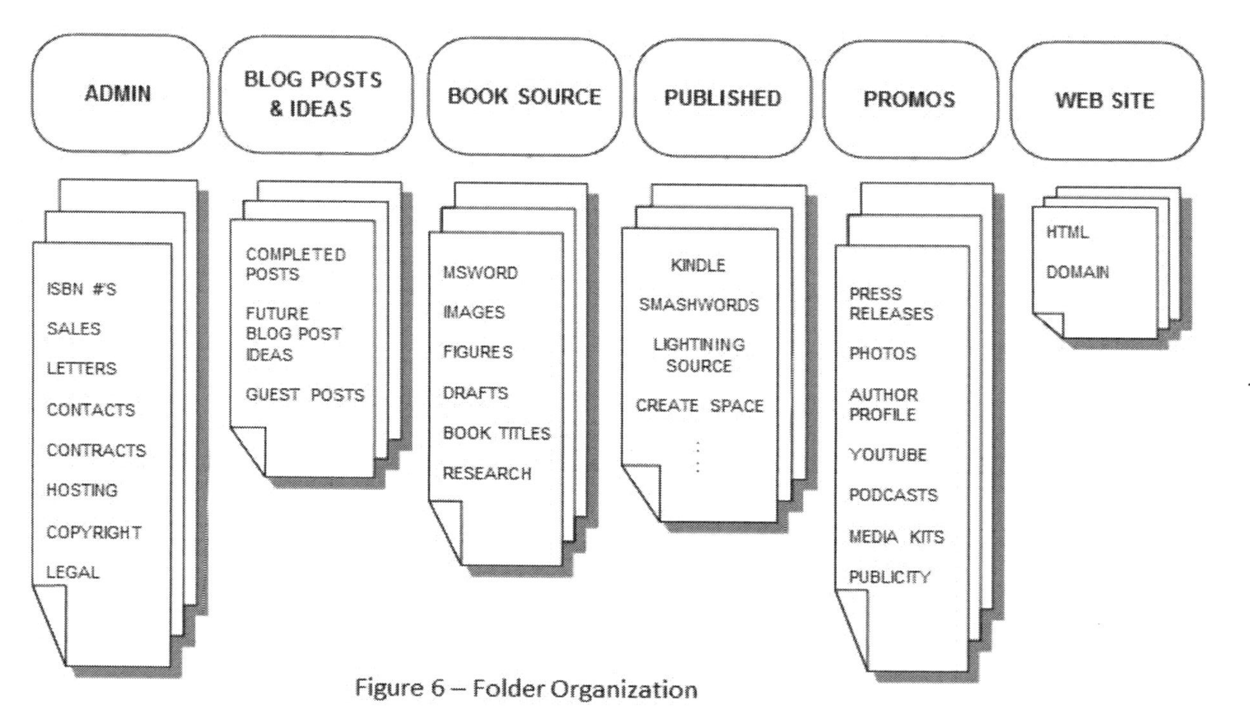

Figure 6 – Folder Organization

The blog posts and the ideas folder is something you will be maintaining to market and sell your book. You will be using this as an idea folder to collect information on blog posts that will attract customers to your blog. Another important folder is your book source, which has all the book content and the bulk of your thinking and effort. The published folder will contain the various published editions for different eBook formats. You also want to keep a promo folder with information for reviewers about your book and author profiles. It is important to save high quality images for your book in your media kit for publicity purposes. Save promotional videos for YouTube and podcasts that you have developed for marketing purposes in the promo folder. If you also have a website, use the website folder to store source information required to create your website.

Backup your web properties

As you go through this book, you will create a number of personal web pages and accounts so make sure you save the web addresses and password hints in safe place. Some of the assets will include a Blogger account, Twitter, Facebook, YouTube, Smashwords, Amazon KDP account,

PayPal account and other online assets. Keep a list of these sites with password hints for each one.

Finally, backup the entire book folder regularly and after each major update. Needless to say, you should save the backup on a different device in a safe place as your book and related material represent many months of work and potential revenue.

STEP 2: YOUR MARKETING PLAN

Once you understand your customers, you will be in a good position to develop a book title, description and identify search keywords your readers may use. Think about who will buy your book and why. How will you reach customers to let them know your book is available?

As an author, you are your brand, whether you use a pen name, company name or your real name. A brand is your identity, encapsulated in how you define yourself online. For example, if you are a fiction writer who writes

Westerns, you may describe yourself as "A Western Fiction Author." What you write about online becomes your brand, your online identity. If your material is targeted to your readers on Facebook, Twitter and your blog, you will attract readers and turn them into buyers.

The bookstore buy decision

In my writers group someone asked the question "Will my book sell?" This is the question every aspiring author wants answered. Just because you publish a book, does not mean it will sell unless you are a known author. There are tens of thousands of authors vying for attention in this crowded space. Putting up a web page, a Facebook page, and a Twitter account does not guarantee sales. However if you have both a great book that resonates with readers and a well-designed marketing strategy you will have a winner.

The reader walks into a bookstore and sees the display as he or she enters the store. The reader is then visually assaulted with magnificent book covers of strategically placed books. As the reader navigates the maze of book displays, book spines and bookshelves, he or she is attracted by the cover design and the title. Once attracted to the book, the reader will pick the book and browse. If reader likes the contents, he or she will keep it and perhaps even make it to the cashier and purchase the book. Let's break the purchase decision down:

- Curiosity - Call to read based on a review or recommendation
- Action - Enter the bookstore
- Attraction - Attracted by the book cover
- Interest - Likes the book title, browses the subtitle and the back cover
- Appeal - Browses the contents and a few text segments
- Commit - Makes the decision to buy

The attributes that come into play are curiosity, action, attractiveness, interest, appeal and commitment to purchase. There may be other things like the feel of the book cover, the texture of the paper or even the smell of the new book. These are the tactile senses that may subconsciously influence the reader.

The online buy decision

As a self-publisher, think about the same behavior on the internet except that the reader is now browsing on the internet and cannot touch, smell or feel the book. Similar attributes come into play online:

- Curiosity - Call to read from your blog post, a review or an online reference
- Action - The buyer lands on your blog and reads your post
- Attraction – Attracted to the book cover
- Interest - Clicks on your book image displayed on the side bar
- Appeal - Browses the contents and sample chapters
- Commit - Makes the decision to buy

The Amazon Kindle eBook website emulates the same book browsing behavior. When a browser lands on the Amazon site, he or she does a search and Amazon displays some books. The book that catches the customer's eye first is the closest match to his or her search keywords. When the customer clicks on that book, Amazon displays

"Frequently Bought Together" books and "Customers Who Bought This Item Also Bought" books. The digital book cover image is not very big on the website or the Kindle device, so the title and subtitle need to be clear and the cover appealing. In addition, the user may be scrolling the website very fast so your cover has to be eye catching. You have less than two seconds to grab the browsers attention with:

- The Cover
- The Title
- Subtitle
- Table of Contents (for non-fiction)
- Sample Chapters

These 5 attributes are as important as the online strategies you will discover in this book. Your keywords and blog topics will be derived from your title, subtitle, promise to the reader, table of contents and introduction. The quality of introduction and sample chapters will sell your book. These need to engage and convince the reader to buy once they click on the book image on Amazon.com or any other online partner store.

Develop your online marketing plan

This section is designed to help you develop your own custom book-marketing plan. The benefit of completing the questions in this section is that you will have the information to:

- Identify your reader interests (profile.)
- Develop subjects for your blog to attract readers.
- Brand yourself on Twitter, Facebook and other social media tools.
- Design your online campaign.
- Identify keywords for your book pages on Amazon and other retail sites

Review the following section and write down the answers for your book. This information will be the key to your online sales and marketing strategy. On completion, you will have a better understanding of your market and the kind of searches your customers conduct.

Book titles

The title must grab the readers' attention and describe your book. The keywords in the title will be the most frequent search on the internet. Do an online search using Google or Yahoo on your book titles and the search keywords you have developed. Do not be surprised or discouraged if your book title exists already. If it exists, just modify it and make it better. When I was writing my book, I must have come up with at least 20 titles, which I can now use as online keywords or develop blog posts around them. If your title is unique and your book has a description based on buyer keywords, it will be more likely to be found by search engines. Change it if the title keywords show up in too many search results, otherwise your book will be hard to find on the search results page.

Book subtitles

The subtitle will be the keywords that will be used when searching for your book on the internet, in addition sites such as Amazon will use the subtitle keywords to display your book to browsers on their site.

Book description

The online description that customers will see on retail book sites is designed to convince the reader to look inside and purchase the book. Describe the benefits and what the reader will discover by reading your book. If you write novels, compose a short enticing description of your book. Is your book on travel, mountain climbing, or science fiction? Think of keywords to engage the reader. This short description will show up on your book retail pages on Amazon, iBooks, Barnes & Noble, Google and others. The keywords in this description will also be tagged in search engines.

Who will read your book?

Think about all possible audiences for your book, what are their age groups, their demographics? Are they farmers, pilots, history buffs, or fiction readers? Imagine what they do and what they may read. If possible, meet your readers in person and get to know them. While writing this book, I joined writers groups and attended self-publisher conferences. For example, if you are a science fiction writer there may be science fiction clubs and online forums where you can engage readers. Goodreads has a book promotion forum on:

http://www.goodreads.com/group/show/55643.Book_Promotion_Forum_by_Genre

Search keywords

The search keywords you develop will be used as tags in your author pages, in your tweets, Facebook posts and blog articles. Write all keywords combinations related to your book that come to mind. These keywords will attract readers.

Competition and research

Find the bestsellers in your category on Amazon.com. Scroll to the bottom of the Amazon book page and see how they rank. Review the bestseller author pages on Amazon and study the keywords they use. Look at the introduction, sample chapters, and see how readers are engaged. What makes your book different from the ones you have found? Write down what your book provides that the others do not.

Google Alerts work to keep you informed by finding new information on your topic. Set up at least one alert with your book title and one with keywords in your subtitle. Use Google Alerts to receive emails about conversations on the internet related to your book. You can set up Google Alerts on **http://www.google.com/alerts**

Where to find your readers?

Although this may be difficult to do, it is worthwhile to think about where you may find your readers and how you may promote your book. For example, if your book is about how to write your memoirs, your readers may be found at specific events.

How can you get more exposure for your book beyond the online strategy described in this book? Are there talks, readings and workshops you can give that target your readers? Search for blogs and online magazines you can submit articles to.

Promotion calendar

Are there special times during the year your book may sell more copies? For example, is your book on holiday decorations or turkey recipes? Is your book about summer travel or spring gardens? Is your book about horror (Friday the 13th or Halloween)? Be prepared with articles for your Tweets, Facebook and blog posts well ahead of these dates. This is part of your ongoing campaign.

Blog topics

Search engines such as Google, Yahoo and Bing will find the keywords and display your blog posts. Search engines like blogs that are active and updated frequently. Over time, you will accumulate content on your blogs, which will cast a wide net for your customers. Focus on the blog topics that serve your customers interests by providing them free information that is of interest to them. Customers are precious, treat them well and do not spam them with a lot of flashy advertisements. Instead, give them information they want to draw them to your website and blog. Based on what you know about your customers, write down blog topics they may be interested in.

Start developing ideas and rough drafts of these blog topics. Blog posts should be no longer than 250 words. Keep a separate blog ideas document and write whenever you feel inspired. You will need these blog ideas in step 5, when you execute your marketing campaign.

Sample chapters

Design sample chapters to have quality information leaving the reader wanting more. Write the first paragraph to engage and entice your reader to read further. Typically, the sample chapters are the first few pages of your book (about 20% of your entire book.) When the title, book description, and sample chapters are well designed, it turns reader curiosity to interest, and interest into a purchase. The book needs to demonstrate value to the book browser. Sample chapters will also show up on internet keyword searches.

Pricing

If your Kindle eBook is priced between USD 2.99 and 9.99 on Amazon you get a 70% royalty, otherwise your royalty drops to 35%. The price table below shows 3 prices at $9.99, $10 and $19.98.

If you sell 100 books at $9.99, you get back 70% or $699.30 in royalties. However if you increase the price by one cent to $10, you get a reduced return of 35% or $350 back for a 100 books sold! To make the same amount as $9.99 for a 100 books you would need to sell your book for at least $19.98.

Price USD $	Authors Royalty	Books Sold	Author Profit USD $
9.99	**0.70**	**100**	**699.30**
		1,000	6,993.00
		10,000	69,930.00
10.00	**0.35**	**100**	**350.00**
		1,000	3,500.00
		10,000	35,000.00
19.98	**0.35**	**100**	**699.30**
		1,000	6,993.00
		10,000	69,930.00

Using this royalty model, Amazon encourages you to keep your price between $2.99 and $9.99.

eBook cover design

The image for "Stories from Things" was licensed from cutcaster.com for $5.50. A graphic design student did the fonts and cover placements.

Make your book cover look professional. A book cover design can cost as little as $30 and is well worth the money. Some book design considerations:

- On Amazon.com, book covers are small at 1 by 1 inch (depending on monitor size and resolution)
- Make the cover attractive and visually pleasing
- The title should be large enough to read on the cover thumbnail image
- Do not clutter the cover with a lot of color and images

Before engaging a cover designer, have a concept and a sketch of what you want your cover to look like. There are a lot of book cover designers, so take a look at their covers before selecting your designer. Browse stock photo sites such as shutterstock.com and istockphoto.com for images that might work for your book. Book cover and graphic designers are worth the money as they have been schooled in visual communications and composition.

Another buyer path is browsing for a book directly from an eReader device. If the customer has an Amazon Kindle, the title and subtitle must show up in the customer's search keywords.

Inside your eBook

Make sure you include a link to your website or blog inside the book. This link is another way to draw customers to buy future books. Describe what the link to your site will provide and the benefit to the reader. Over time, you may have more books to sell and this link will have your latest books listed on your blog or website. Retailers like Amazon will not release who bought your book. Links are a way to connect with your readers.

Your online brand

Your book is your brand. Develop a consistent brand and logo for your books. Great examples of a brand are the "For Dummies" books and "Chicken Soup for" books. They have a certain look and image that is consistent and trusted. Use the brand words and image consistently across your websites, blogs, business cards, press kits, social media, print books and eBooks. Your book title is also your brand, as is your Twitter icon, Facebook page, blog and website.

About the author

About the author shows up on Amazon below the book cover and below the book description. This is another place to sell your brand. Buyers like to read about the author before they make the purchase. Look at how best sellers in your book category portray themselves and craft yours accordingly.

STEP 3: BUILD YOUR PLATFORM

A platform is a set of tools such as your blog, Twitter account, Facebook page, Amazon book page and other retail book sites used to market and sell your book. Step 3 will show you how to get started with a basic platform and Step 4 will complete your platform by adding your published eBook on retail sites such as iBooks and Amazon.

One author I worked with took several weeks to implement all the steps. He initially set up a blog using

Google Blogger and a Twitter account. This gave him the experience to work with blogs and interact with people on social networks. By creating a blog, he built an online platform to market his work. Being online exposed him to customers and reviewers.

Platform priorities

There are many online tools in this market space. Some are better than others are, some are more powerful but too complex for the non-technical folks. Some tools are more popular in a particular market vertical, demographic and geography.

Your core platform priorities are getting published on Amazon and Smashwords. Followed by a blog and a Twitter account as shown in Figure 7. These are the core tools you need to publish market and sell your book.

Although a Facebook presence is essential for the author, it adds additional value only after the core tools are in place. Step 7 covers other promotional tools such as YouTube videos, Podcasts, Google AdWords, Facebook ads and social bookmarks.

Online Tools x Incremental Value	Highest Value	More Value	Additional Value
Publish eBook on Amazon & Smashwords	Step 4		
Blog and Twitter	Step 3		
Facebook		Step 3	
Publish on Demand (POD) Print Book		Step 3	
Promo Video (YouTube, Animoto, Vimeo, SlideShare, and others)			Step 7
Social Bookmarking			Step 7
Podcasts on Apple iTunes & Other Sites			Step 7
Google AdWords, Facebook Ads			Step 7

Figure 7 – Online Tools Value and Priorities Chart

This book does not pick one tool over another, rather it chooses the simplest way for non-technical authors to get started with eBook publishing. Google Blogger, Facebook and Twitter will get you started with your basic eBook sales and marketing platform.

Once you have set up your platform, it takes no more than half an hour a day to manage your network. All you need to do is post a small article (about 250 words) on your blog at least once a week and be active on Twitter.

Rapid and simple blog setup

Blogger is straightforward, use the link below to create your blog:

- Go to **http://www.blogger.com** and sign on (you will need an email account.)
- Go to "Create a Blog" and give it a name, use your book title or some combination of your keywords. Blogger will let you know if the blog address (URL) is available.

- Enter a blog title. You can always go back and change this title at a later date.
- Enter the address, in this case it is "The7StepEBook"

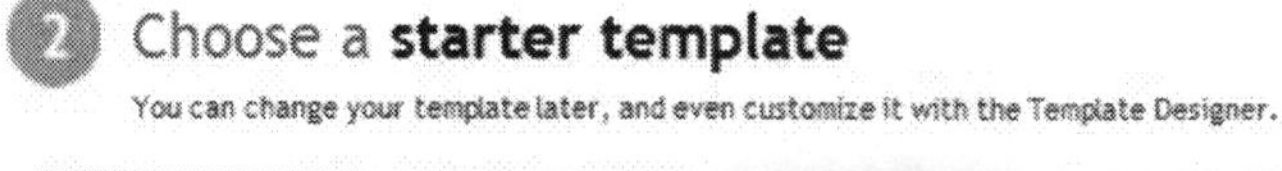

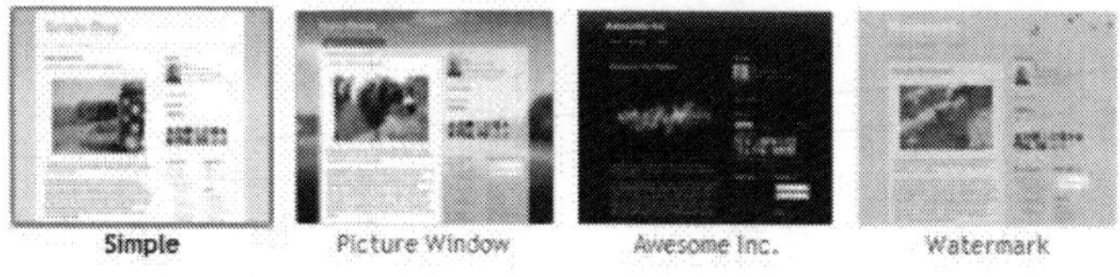

Google Blogger has some great starter blog templates; select a simple one or if you are lucky choose a template that relates to your book theme. Keep your blog simple and not too busy. The purpose of your blog is to sell books and provide valuable information to your customer.

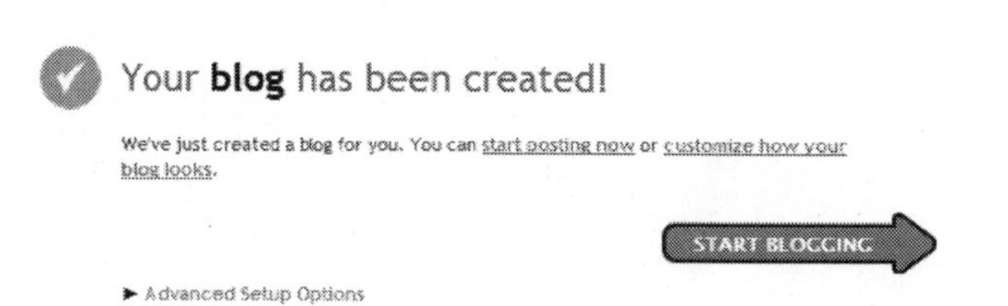

Now that you have created a blog, create your first post. Make yourself familiar with the icons on the toolbar. For example, you can use the picture icon to add a picture on your post and the "Link" menu item to add links to your post. Just try it; you can always delete it later if you like.

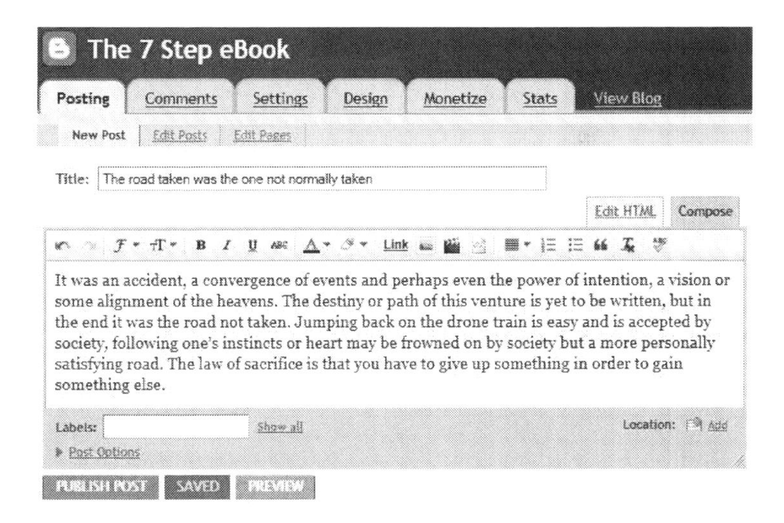

Now "Publish Post" and view your blog. That's it; you have set up your blog and published your first post.

Add navigation pages to Blogger

On your blog add "About the author" and "About the book" navigation buttons. Do this by selecting the

"Postings" tab followed by the "Edit Pages" tab and select add a "New Page."

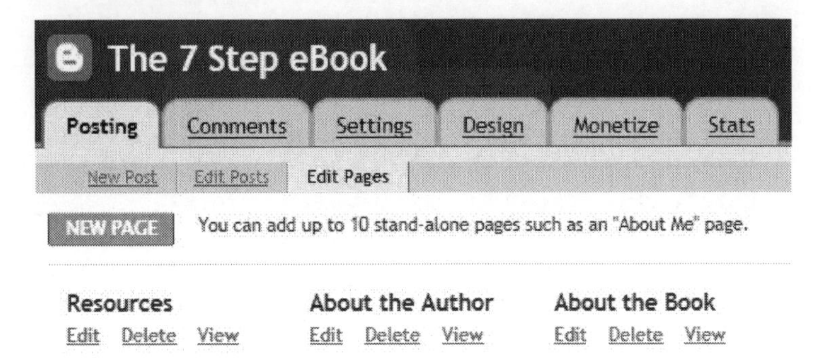

Tips on Google Blogger

Add **http://blogspot.com/** to your favorites bar so it is easily available. On the Settings tab, under:

- "Who Can Comment?" select "Anyone." This will encourage blog visitors to comment as anonymous.
- "Comment Moderation" select "Never" and the comments will be posted up right away without any moderation. It is gratifying to blog visitors to see their comments appear instantly. If offending comments ever become a problem, you can always delete them and turn on moderation by selecting "Always." Over time as your blog becomes more popular you may need comment moderation re-enabled.

- "Show word verification for comments?" select "No" for now. If spam becomes a problem, you may turn it back on. A lot of users just exit the word verification step and as a result, no comments are left.

Under the Comments tab:

- Review your comments once a day and respond. Delete inappropriate ones, if any.

Add an automatic signature on your email to include a link and promote your blog.

Twitter setup and branding

If you have not already setup a Twitter account, this may be the right time to work on it. Twitter is an effective marketing tool to drive traffic to your website. Visit **http://twitter.com** to sign up by entering your name, email and password on the signup screen. Twitter will walk you through a simple setup wizard to get you started.

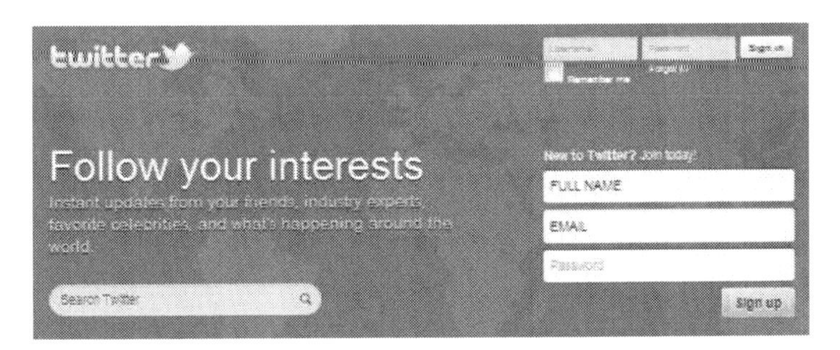

Twitter setup is straightforward, the important setup items are:

- your user name
- your picture
- profile bio

These will define your Twitter brand as discussed in Step 2. Your Twitter user name will be your online identity. Upload either your picture or the picture of your logo that is consistent across your websites and eBooks. I suggest using your full name or your company name. Twitter also lets you describe a profile bio in 160 characters or less. Set it up for now as you can always modify it later. , if you need help go to the Twitter support site at:

http://support.twitter.com , or search YouTube for videos on the subject.

Example Twitter profile

Sadiq Somjee

@GeoEdgePub Vancouver, Canada

How to publish, sell and market eBooks for authors new to this stuff. I am a family man who has been in the tech industry for 20+ years.

http://the7stepebook.blogspot.com/

This profile is 136 characters with spaces; it took some tweaking to shorten it. I like to use Word to write my profile as it has a character count feature. How does your online identity contribute to your brand and credibility? Take a look how other authors and artists describe themselves on Twitter. The Twitter profile bio has a 160-character limitation, because it forces one to play with words and sentences to make an effective pitch. Imagine that you have 2 seconds to describe yourself to a customer before the elevator door opens. Think of what you would say with a smile on your face. Does your profile bio, picture and user name have the hook to get a viewer to click on your Twitter profile and link to your blog?

Sign on to your Twitter account at **http://twitter.com** and tweet.

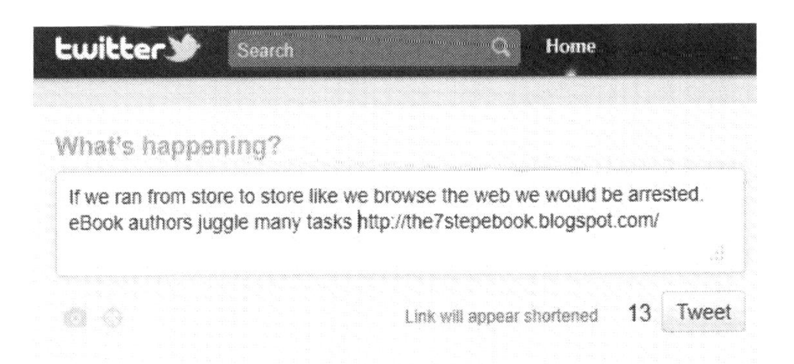

Notice the http link back to your blog posts. That's how you drive visitors to your website. Are your tweets engaging? Does the tag line leave the reader curious enough to click on your link?

A word on spamming

One form of spamming is excessive self-promotion and another common one is getting people on a website busy with ads and little content. Spamming guarantees that your readers will get frustrated and "unfollow" you. Build your Twitter reputation by providing valuable information, sharing information from others by "re-tweeting" their tweets and over time you will build a following based on trust and credibility. Based on the information developed in Step 2, ask yourself if you are giving your readers the information they want.

Tips on Twitter

- On the top menu bar click on, "Messages," check your messages daily and reply.
- Find people to follow by clicking on "Who to Follow" and select "Browse Interests."

- You can also enter a category such "author" to search for authors. Join people, groups, magazines and organizations where your customers may hang out as identified in Step 2.
- Create Lists, you can list twitter accounts and people can choose to follow the list. Be strategic on your lists based on your marketing plan.

- Retweet something you like by clicking on *Retweet.* If you promote others, they will promote you. Do this carefully and honestly to build your credibility over time.
- Use the @name tag to direct a comment to someone on Twitter. Type "@" and then type their username. This will appear on their feed regardless if they follow you or not.
- If you want to get the attention of "memoir" writers in your tweet, use the "#" tag. For example, "Announcing my memory objects #memoir show at the #Portland

Art Gallery, reception October 15 at 6pm. Show also online at **http://storiesfromthings.blogspot.com**." Notice how I tagged Portland to hook the locals and plugged the book blog at the same time.

Tips on how to make search engines happy

- What you enter in the "Title" and "Labels" field in Blogger is what Google will pick up as search keywords. Once Google or Yahoo has scanned your blog, your post will show up in searches. The rank of the post depends on the uniqueness, the activity on your blog, the keyword combinations and links to your post.
- Linking to other websites, will make search engines happy and give you a better search ranking
- The more frequently you post, the happier Google, Yahoo and other search engines will be.
- In addition, the more comments and interaction you get on your blog, the better. Engage readers and always follow up.

Facebook Author Page

There are several options on how to create an author presence on Facebook. One way is to create a group page. Group pages allow you as the administrator more control over who joins the group and you can ban or remove members from your group. The problem with group pages is that they limit the number of members you can have. I do not recommend group pages for authors unless you are creating an exclusive membership club. Instead, I do recommend creating a Facebook Author Page. Like a business page, it is available to everyone on Facebook and thus very public. It will also be listed on search engines so people can discover you and your book.

If you do not already have a personal Facebook account, create one now on:

http://www.Facebook.com

Your Facebook account is typically personal for close friends and family, while your Facebook Author Page will be public. This really depends on whether you want your Facebook to be open to the public. I prefer to have a separate private profile and a public Author Page. Login to your Facebook account and set up your Author Page:

http://www.Facebook.com/pages/create.php

Select the "Artist, Band, or Public Figure" option; alternatively, if you operate under a company you can select company option. Under your page option select "Author" from the drop down box and name your page. Your page name can be your book name, your name or your pen name.

Artist, Band or Public Figure
Join your fans on Facebook.

Author

My Book Name

I agree to Facebook Pages Terms

Get Started

Upload your profile photo or brand. On "The 7 Step eBook" page, I used the book cover to brand my Facebook page; this brand is consistent with my Twitter profile and the book cover image on my blog.

Customize your Facebook Author Page with your book information developed in Step 2. Provide your basic information such as your pitch, endorsements and your back cover material developed in step 2. Promote your page by adding a "LIKE" button. Later you can add relevant material such as videos, slides, and images as you develop them.

Link Facebook to Twitter

On your Facebook Author Page, select "Resources" from the left menu and select "Link your Page to Twitter." If you are asked to switch back to your personal page, approve it and proceed to link your Page to Twitter. This way when you publish a post on your Facebook Author Page, it will automatically show up on Twitter.

Test Facebook, Twitter and Blogger

Test how Facebook, Twitter and Blogger all work in harmony. Go to your "Wall" on Facebook and update your status box with a link to your blog by copying the post address (URL) on your browser. This will broadcast the message to your Facebook followers, Twitter followers and link to your blog with one action.

Another way to broadcast a message is to sign on to Facebook and have your Author Page open in your browser, open a new browser tab with your blog and click on the Facebook button below your blog post. Your blog post will be shared to Facebook and Twitter at the same time.

Summary

In this chapter, you set up a blog, Twitter and a Facebook Author Page. You also completed your first blog post and shared it on Facebook and Twitter with one action. Now you have an idea of how your platform works together. Keep practicing to become competent and make it a routine.

STEP 4: PUBLISH YOUR EBOOK & PRINT BOOK

This chapter introduces the Publish 1-2-3 system. This system is a simple method to publish and distribute your work to multiple eReaders and to a print book.

Publish 1-2-3 system

The 3 key publishing streams described cover a wide distribution for your eBook across online bookstores and eReader devices. The beauty of this system is that you can do this with one master word proccesing document as shown in Figure 8.

(1) The Amazon Kindle stream. By publishing via Kindle Direct Publishing (KDP) on Amazon, your eBook will be available on the Kindle and a number of other eReaders supported by Amazon.

To buy a Kindle eBook, the reader must buy it from Amazon and not the other retailers. The solution to gain maximum exposure for your book is to publish it to multiple devices and online book retailers using Smashwords.

(2) The Smashwords stream. By publishing with Smashwords, your eBook will be made available to a number of online bookstores and devices including the iPad, Nook, Sony and Kobo. Smashwords distributes your eBook to major retailers such Apple, Barnes & Noble and Chapters.

(3) The POD stream publishes a print copy via CreateSpace. The avantage of CreateSpace is that it is owned by Amazon, which lists your book on Amazon. Many authors use Lighting Source which is owned by Ingram. Both are good options.

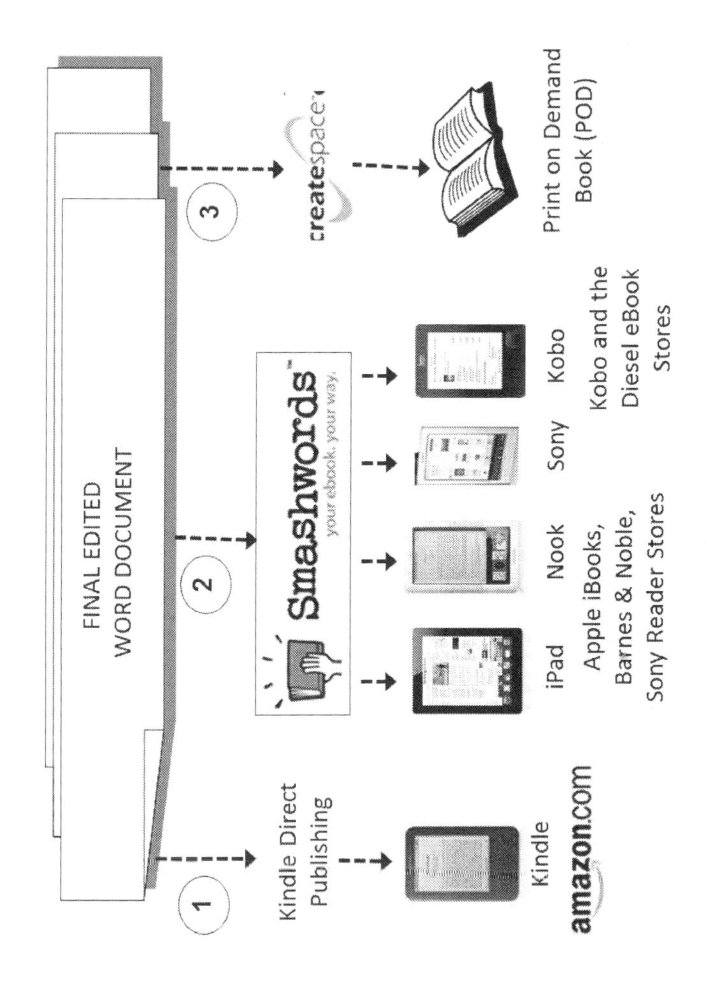

Figure 8 – Publish 1-2-3

Review of steps completed

In Step 2, we developed a marketing plan, got an understanding of your readers and developed a brand around the book. In Step 3, we built a blog, set up a Facebook page and a branded Twitter profile. An attractive book cover design and a catchy book title were developed to be clearly visible on the one-inch Amazon.com thumbnail.

Publishing is more than a mechanical process of getting your book into an eBook format, it requires developing a marketing plan, building an online publishing, marketing and selling platform and keeping active on social media.

(1) The Amazon Kindle stream

Start by making a backup copy of your manuscript, as you will be changing the format and layout of your document. Your book needs to be formatted to Kindle specifications in order display on the Kindle, there are several ways to do this, and all you need to do is choose <u>one</u> of the following methods that you are comfortable with:

1. The simplest approach is to use Microsoft Word. If you are familiar with Word, this is your best option. Amazon recommends this method as well.

2. Publish using HTML. Select this method if you do not have Microsoft Word and your word processor can "Save As" HTML.

3. Publish using a PDF or a text file.

4. If you are an Adobe InDesign user, Amazon provides a "plug-in" to convert your book into the Kindle format.

Using MS Word to publish can save you a lot of formatting grief and is worth the purchase. However, there are a number of word processing options available. If your word processor can save to web format (HTML), it should work. One option is the free "Writer" word processor from Open Office. Open Office provides software for word processing, spreadsheets, presentations, and graphics. You can download Open Office from:

http://www.openoffice.org/

Writer lets you open and save files in various formats including Word and HTML.

To publish your book you will need:

- Title and subtitle as developed in Step 2
- Book cover image from Step 2 (JPEG)
- Front matter (title, copyright, dedication, preface and prologue)
- Back matter (bibliographies, appendices, glossaries if needed)

Formatting guidelines

eBooks do not work like print books, so do not bother with special fonts, spacing, tabs and line breaks. You will need two versions of your manuscript one formatted one for print and one with simple formatting for an eBook. Since eReaders have different screen sizes there are no page numbers. The readers of these devices rely on features such as hyperlinks to jump to a location and electronic bookmarks.

The conversion of a Word document to a Kindle eBook works well without much effort. Word features such as bolding text, italics, page breaks, text alignment and headings all come out well on the Kindle. For the most part, the Amazon conversion process is simple and straightforward. The Amazon Kindle Direct Publishing (KDP) site provides good documentation and video tutorials. There is also an active online community where you can ask for help if you run into specific issues. You can find the links on **http://www.7StepEBook.com** under resources.

The images will shrink to fit the little Kindle screen so make sure the images are clear and the text is large. Testing images will take some trial and error before you get it right. Images need to be centered in Word as you would center text. You can preview your test eBook without publishing it on the Amazon KDP site using the preview tool described later in this section.

Color images will show up better on color devices such as the iPad and the color Nook. My recommendation is to keep color images, as it will make your eBook visually attractive on the color Kindle Fire and on other eReaders such as the color Nook. Most color images will also display fine on older gray scale eReaders.

Enter two returns and a page break at the end of every chapter to ensure that the chapters are displayed separately on non-Kindle devices using EPUB formats (such as the Sony Reader, Kobo, Nook, Stanza, Adobe Digital Editions and others.)

Before you start formatting your document, it is important you familiarize yourself with the style guide available free on Smashwords.com. Even though your document may look good on a Kindle, it will not show up well on Kindle reading applications for iPad, iPhone, PC and other devices. If you do not follow the Smashwords style guide, your document will have chapters sticking to the last line of the last chapter, your table of contents will lose its alignment and your paragraphs will have different styles. This means people who download your book on non-kindle devices from Amazon will have a poor reading experience and will not enjoy reading the book.

The nice thing about publishing on Amazon is that you can keep uploading and previewing your versions until you get it right before you publish.

Take a look at the "Simplified Guide to Building a Kindle Book" under "Types of Formats" on:

https://kdp.amazon.com/self-publishing/help

Note web links from sites such as Amazon may be updated and may not work; if this is the case go to the 7 Step eBook site for updated links under the resources page:

http://www.7stepeBook.com

Kindle publishing steps

Verify that, the front of the book content, such as copyrights, acknowledgements, placeholder title and the ISBN (You do not need an ISBN for Amazon) is in your Word document. In a nutshell, these are the Word to Amazon Kindle publishing steps:

(a) Convert your Word document to HTML by using the SAVE AS Web page FILTERED command in Word.

(b) Use MobiPocket to covert the HTML file to a *.prc extension file (more on this in the next few pages.)

(c) Set up your account on **https://kdp.amazon.com** if you have not already done so.

(d) Go to your bookshelf, select "add a new title", and fill in the required information.

(e) Pay particular attention to the how you fill in "Target your book to customers" section. You will be allowed to select two book categories and seven search keywords. This information is how your readers will find your book on Amazon. Search keywords were developed in Step 2, your marketing plan.

(f) Upload the book cover image as specified by Amazon. (JPEG minimum 500 pixels wide by a maximum of 1280 pixels long, saved at 72 dots per inch (dpi))

(g) Upload the MobiPocket file (.prc extension) on Amazon.

(h) Preview the eBook draft online on Amazon. On the website select Bookshelf and on the "Actions" tab select "Edit book details." Scroll to the bottom of the page and select preview book.

(i) Look at the preview on Amazon.com and your Word document side by side. Make the corrections on your local Word document. This approach will keep your Word document as the pristine master copy.

(j) Correct your Word document and repeat steps (a), (b), (g), (h) and (i) until you are satisfied with how your book looks on the Amazon online preview. Tip: Delete any previous .HTML and .prc extension files and directories created by MobiPocket before starting step (a) again. You will find these files a directory called "MyPublications"

(k) Finally, enter a price for your book and release it for sale on Amazon.

I started with the Amazon Kindle first, because it is the simplest and has a wide distribution. If you have spent some time and reviewed the Smashwords Style guide, I suggest you start with Smashwords and aim to get on their premier catalogue. This way you will have a well-formatted Word document to publish on Amazon. Painful as it may seem, the Smashwords review process works well and is worth the effort.

Publishing tools

Now that you have read the, "Kindle Publishing Steps", you are probably wondering how to get and use the tools mentioned. This section explains how to use publishing tools and where to get them online. In step (b), the Word file needs to be converted into the Kindle format using either the MobiPocket tool or the Calibre tool. Download and install “MobiPocket Creator Home Edition” under the “Software” tab from **http://www.mobipocket.com**

MobiPocket Creator lets you import Word, HTML, text, or PDF files and convert them in the Kindle format. Note that MobiPocket only works for PC’s and not for Mac’s or Linux computers. Skip ahead to the Calibre tool section if you have a Mac or a Linux computer.

From Word export your document to HTML (filtered) and then use MobiPocket to import the HTML file. Select “HTML Document” and import the HTML file. Do not bother adding the cover image, or metadata. This information will not be transferred to Amazon online.

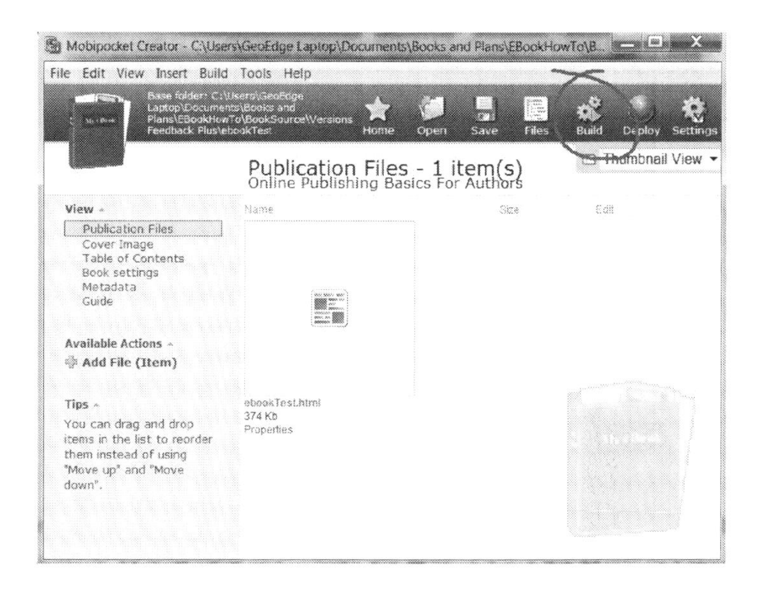

After importing your document, convert it using the "Build" button. The resulting output may then be dragged into the Kindle Preview desktop tool for proofing.

The Mac alternative to MobiPocket is **Calibre**. However, Calibre does not accept Word, so you will need to save your document as a HTML file to convert your book to the Kindle Mobi format. Calibre is available for the Mac, Linux and Windows systems, while MobiPocket only works for Windows.

http://www.calibre-eBook.com/download

On the Calibre menu click on "Add books" and select your file in a supported format such as HTML, TXT, PDF or

ODT and click "Convert books." In the pop up window, select the output format as, "mobi." Once it has converted, select "Save to disk." Upload the resulting file to Amazon [step (g)].

One of the nice features of the Calibre tool is that it lets you save the file directly to the Kindle device. If you own a Kindle, it is worth looking at how the book will appear on the device and how the reader will experience your book. Take a look at how some other books are formatted for ideas. To save your book on your Kindle device from Calibre, simply plug it in to the USB port and Calibre will allow you to save to it. The Kindle device is seen as a storage unit and you can add or delete your eBook like any other storage drive.

The Kindle Previewer emulates how books display on Kindle Devices and applications. It will display the formatted eBook (.prc file) the way the Kindle reader sees it for orientation, font size and text display. The Kindle Previewer is good to use if you do not have a physical Kindle device as it does simulate the real Kindle reasonably well.

http://www.amazon.com/kindlepublishing

Scroll to the bottom of the page and search for "Download Kindle Previewer." After downloading and installing the Previewer, open the file with the .prc extension saved with MobiPocket. Correct any mistakes in your original Word document, convert your book, and preview until your book looks acceptable. The Kindle Previewer tool is optional as the online preview described in (h) is all you need.

Online resources

Amazon has a good video tutorial on the KDP site under the menu. On the KDP website select (1) Publish Your Book -> (2) Getting Started -> (3) How To Publish – Video Tutorial or go to the resources section on

https://kdp.amazon.com or on

http://www.the7stepeBook.com

See the Amazon help site for guidelines:

https://kdp.amazon.com/self-publishing/help

(2) The Smashwords Stream

By placing your book on Smashwords your book is exposed to thousands of readers, it provides additional search engine visibility for your eBook. Like Amazon, it is a portal for readers to land and spend time browsing books. Smashwords allows authors to enter keywords for search engines to find your book. These are the keywords you developed in Step 2, your marketing plan to attract the right customers. The information you enter will be sent to the retail sites where Smashwords distributes.

Although you have your blog or website, Smashwords has a higher search visibility than your blog because it has a community of authors and publishers like any online bookstore. Other authors and even competitive books create this watering hole for readers to stop and take a drink, which is essentially the visibility you want for your book. This is also true when you publish your book on sites such as Amazon. In addition to increasing your book visibility, Smashwords has periodic marketing campaigns, ongoing SEO optimization and coupon programs to help promote your book. The Smashwords company relationship with the author is symbiotic as its success is tied to the author's success.

Smashwords.com provides excellent eBook conversion and distribution services. Since Smashwords.com provides good documentation under the "FAQ" page, I will not repeat what is already on their site, but I will provide an overview and some key points to help you get published with them.

Smashwords takes your Word document and converts it into several eBook formats including formats for the iPad, Nook, Sony and Kobo. Smashwords also takes care of the distribution network of retailers including Apple, Barnes & Noble, Sony, Kobo and others. Authors retain 85% (or in other words Smashwords keeps 15%) of the net sale proceeds of their books, a small price to pay for the conversion and retail distribution of eBooks. The author proceeds vary depending on the country, retailer and often on the eBook pricing. For example, as of this writing Apple and Barnes & Noble return 60% to the author. Everyone in the chain gets a small cut, I see this as a win/win proposal, the author gets the book published, Smashwords provides the distribution to multiple retailers, and the retailers get a cut. For example, if Apple keeps 40%, Smashwords takes 15% of the remaining 60% then the author gets 51%. If you participate in the Smashwords affiliate program, it will cost you an additional 11% of net sales (i.e. 51 %). That works out to 45% back in your pocket, still higher than the traditional publisher model. Imagine being listed on Apple iTunes and Barnes & Noble, these retailers have huge online traffic volumes. This is an opportunity to get amazing exposure for your eBook. Please refer to the Smashwords.com site to get the latest and specific author royalty formula details.

Keep in mind that Amazon has no agreement with Smashwords as of this writing and since you have published directly via the Amazon KDP program, your Amazon Kindle eBook proceeds come directly from Amazon. As an author, I prefer this because currently Amazon has the largest eBook market share. If you price your eBook between $2.99 and $9.99 in North America, you retain 70% of the proceeds. As an author, I obviously prefer readers to buy from Amazon; however, readers will buy from anywhere they want because of brand loyalties and device convenience. For example, Apple enthusiasts with iPads will buy from iBooks and you will get 45% after all the middlemen take their cut. If you have difficulty with that, the other option is to use the Calibre tool and publish directly to online books stores individually. The problem is that some online bookstores like Chapters will not accept books from Indies, but they have an agreement with

Smashwords. It is also a fair amount of work to manage all the online bookstores and marketing, so if you like the one stop shop publishing, Smashwords is the way to go. It provides publishing, distribution and marketing services for the indie author.

I like a couple of clauses in Smashwords contract, as of this writing (1) the author has the right to remove their work from Smashwords at any time and (2) the author retains the copyright. This is similar to the Amazon KDP contract.

Smashwords helps you market your book by providing a web page for your eBook and also offers an affiliate program. By joining the affiliate program, third party bloggers, internet marketers, authors, website operators and publishers promote your book for a percentage (11%) of net sales. You have the option to join or opt out of the affiliate program at any time. I would join this program because it gives your books more exposure and rewards the affiliates for the promotion. Aim for exposure and wide distribution initially, when you see your sales picking up, you may review your partnerships. If it works for you don't change it, just do more of the same.

Format your eBook on Smashwords

Although Smashwords accepts Microsoft Word and Open Office Writer formats, Word is recommended. Open Office Writer can save files as .DOC (Word format), however, Writer introduces a number of formatting problems. Download Smashwords Style Guide; if you cannot find it on the site go to resources page on:

http://www.the7stepeBook.com/

Reading the Smashwords Style Guide is a must, do not skip this step. It provides information to publish your book successfully and it gets listed on their premier catalog. If you are having trouble formatting, Smashwords will provide a list of people who will format your book for a reasonable fee ranging from $30 to $50 depending on the complexity of your book. Formatting your book can be cumbersome and I would be happy to pay someone to do this for me next time. The advantage of learning how to format is that you can update your eBook as you please without cost each time.

Getting paid

Retailers such as Smashwords require a PayPal account so that they can pay you. Go to **https://www.paypal.com** sign up and link your bank account. The approval and validation process takes about 2 or 3 days.

Other options

Recently I heard of a new service by BookBaby.com, although I have not tried it out, it may be good option for those authors who want to farm out all their work. The online reviews have been good. The advantage with BookBaby is that for a small fee ($99) they will convert your book from just about any format and publish it to Amazon, Barnes & Noble, Apple and Sony. Bookbaby does not charge a commission, instead it charges a flat fee whether your book sells or not. It also provides additional services like cover design and formating. Unlike Smashwords their book conversion process is not automated and everything is done manually by their staff. The disavantage is that if you want to correct errors and modify your book on the fly, you need to go through the process again. BookBaby accepts a number of formats ranging from Word, Adobe InDesign, Text, PDF, Quark and others. BookBaby's sister companies Like HostBaby provide author website services and CDbaby provides audio book services. Regardless of the service you use, your online marketing through social media and blogs is still important.

(3) Publish on Demand (POD) stream

Having a print book is worth the effort, because it expands your customer base. No inventory and low cost specialized print on demand companies is the new model. My young nephew with all the gizmos stopped buying iPad books and switched back to lugging his college textbooks so he could highlight, place yellow stickers, scribble and pencil notes on his print books. On the other hand, my 75-year-old father-in-law who never used a computer before does most of his reading on his iPad. I use this example because print books are not necessarily just for older folks. Print books will be around for a while and the print book market cannot be ignored. The way people buy print books is changing from bookstores to online. Although, I must admit I enjoy browsing physical books in bookstores.

Both Lighting Source and CreateSpace provide good documentation to help you get started with creating print books. Although there are a number of POD printers out there with great services, CreateSpace of Amazon and Lighting Source of Ingram are the two I would recommend. Lighting source is a good choice if you have a small company and are willing to spend around 100 dollars in setup fees and $12 in annual fees to get you listed in Ingram's book distribution databases. I found CreateSpace easier to set up while Lighting Source had more setup procedures and paperwork.

Lighting Source (LSI)

Lighting Source is an independent distributor and produces book catalogs to their distribution partners such as Ingram, Baker & Taylor, Barnes & Noble and Amazon. This makes your book available on demand to all major bookstores; however, bookstores do not carry self-published books. As a self-publisher focus on the online sales of your print book.

LSI distribution

Bookstores, schools and libraries access the book database produced by Ingram. Publishing with Lighting Source gives your book wide exposure and will automatically be listed by online sellers such as Amazon and other third party vendors. Ingram has a distribution network of over 30,000 wholesalers, retailers and bookstores in over 100 countries. Although bookstores do not stock self-published books, the book can be ordered on demand from the Ingram database. This is a good thing because the goal is not to carry costs associated with an inventory of books; the goal is to get your print book listed on Amazon. With, "print to order", your book is printed when a customer buys the book and it is ready for shipment within 12 hours.

POD costs and profit

Since, Lighting Source (LSI) is a publisher; there is only the cost of printing once the book is sold. Your profit is the book price, less the bookstore discount and the printing costs.

LSI has a number of book product choices to select from, assume you select a black and white 5"x8" paperback book product. If your book is 100 pages, costs $2.50 to print and is priced at $10, your profit will be $10 less $2.50 less $2 (20% of the cover price based on the LSI short discount.) This works out to $5.50 back in your pocket. Once the reader purchases the book from Amazon, Amazon will order it from Ingram and Lighting Source will fulfill the order and deposit your dues to your bank account. All you need to do is direct customers to Amazon from your marketing platform and work on your book page keywords (tags) on Amazon.

https://www.lightningsource.com

CreateSpace (An Amazon Company)

In this example, I used CreateSpace for the following benefits:

- CreateSpace is owned by Amazon and has fast turnaround on Amazon.com listings.
- The book is automatically made available on Amazon.com, which means that customer service, shipping and payments are all handled for you.
- Because your book is available on Amazon.com benefits such as providing customers to look inside your book, discounted shipping and other Amazon promotions are automatically available for your print book.
- CreateSpace generates a free ISBN for you.

- By enrolling in the Pro-Plan, you get access to an expanded distribution channel to distribute your book to retailers, bookstores, libraries, wholesalers and distributers. The one time setup fee is $39 and $5 annually thereafter. This is worth the money because you get an expanded distribution and earn higher royalties.

- If you do not want to convert your book for the Kindle, CreateSpace will convert your book for a small fee ($69) and put the Kindle edition on Amazon.com for sale.

- Professional print formatting services are available from $300 to $600 depending on the type of book (Text, Illustrated, or Children's.)

- CreateSpace provides the cover creator tool to generate your book cover automatically from your images and text. For a reasonable fee, CreateSpace will provide a professional designer create a custom cover.

- Word templates for formatting for standard book formats are provided to help you format your book.

- You can purchase your own copies of your book at cost. This is great for proofing your book and acquiring promotion copies.

To get started just sign on to CreateSpace and follow the steps online. **https://www.createspace.com**

Online retail

Ensure that your book information is correct on Amazon.com, Smashwords and elsewhere before proceeding to Step 5.

Why publish to multiple eBook sellers?

First, your eBook will be listed on several online bookstores. Second, you will discourage piracy by making your eBook widely available and the third reason is that the eReader technology is changing so fast that devices are constantly dropping in and out of favor. As of this writing, the Kindle had the largest eBook market share, the color Nook is picking up market share and of course, the iPad will continue to be a significant player.

Other players such as Sony, Kobo, and Google Android tablets are also growing their customer base. For example,

Sony just partnered with J.K Rowling under the Pottermore brand to bring Harry Potter fans eBooks and an online experience. Each one of these devices (eReaders, tablets, mobiles, phones…) will attract a different demographic and the device market share will change periodically.

Customers may have loyalty to a device brand or to a favorite online bookstore. In addition, online bookstores have developed applications to run on the Blackberry Playbook, Samsung Galaxy Android and other gadgets (enough to fill a few pages.) In summary, publishing to multiple eBook retailers will expand your potential customer base, reduce piracy, and protect you from gadget loyalty wars. It turns out that you only need to publish your book at 3 places to access this huge eBook market.

Summary

Step 4 covered the Publish 1-2-3 system, that gets your eBook to all major eReaders and book retailers and gets your print book listed on Amazon using CreateSpace or LSI.

Formatting an eBook is very different from a pBook (print book.) A print book is WYSIWYG, or "What You See Is

What You Get." You can use various fonts, font sizes, styles, and breaks and they will appear in the same way when published. An eBook is rendered differently on eReaders that come in different sizes and have different formatting rules.

This step marks a major milestone in getting published; now you are set to reap the benefits of having a sales platform to sell your eBook and pBook.

STEP 5: EXECUTE YOUR CAMPAIGN

At this point it is worth bringing together some of the ideas on marketing discussed in previous chapters. Recall when you advertise via Twitter or Facebook, you want to hook customers and draw them to look at your book. In this case, the hook is via Twitter to an article of interest to your reader on your blog.

Next, you want your blog to have a *stickiness quality*. In the "Tipping Point," Malcolm Gladwell talks about the *stickiness* of Sesame Street and Blues Clues as the ability to keep the attention of young children watching the shows. Similarly, you want your blog posts to be interesting and valuable to your reader. People typically buy after multiple visits and reminders about the book. Keep active with sticky blog posts. Your blog will have a link and picture of your book on the right hand side. It gives the blog visitor an easy way to get to your online eBook on Amazon, iBooks, or any other online bookstore. According to Wikipedia, "Sticky content on the Web attracts visitors to return to the site and/or spend long periods of time on the same site."

eBooks need to be sticky with a professional cover design, great title, subtitle, description, and reader benefits. These attributes should compel the reader to open and read the table of contents, introduction and sample chapters. As you read Step 5, keep in mind the *stickiness* of your website, blog, online bookstores and tweets.

- **Hook** - Tag lines on your retail book pages
- **Consistent** – Be present with regular tweets and blog posts

- **Attractive** – Simple blog designed for your readers
- **One-click** - link to your book seller
- **Get to the buy** – Cover, title, description, price, and sample chapters

Design your blog to sell

Keep your blog design simple; avoid flashy images and visual distractions. Your blog focus is your book and links to retail sites. Web sites or blogs with a lot of ads and flashing images are annoying and you will lose customers. Stay away from colorful and visually noisy designs. Look at the Google home page for example. It has a lot of white space, not fancy, but the main thing it does is search. Your purpose is to sell books so stay away from flashy ads and keep the website simple. The only thing you want the buyer to see is your blog post with a side link to your book. Modify your blog layout by selecting the "Design" menu in Google Blogger. Add a picture of your book using the "Add a Gadget" button and selecting the "picture" gadget. In your picture gadget upload your book picture and add the link to your book on Amazon. You can add as many picture gadgets as you have resellers. Figure 9 shows an example of a suggested blog layout, the reader is one-click away to the book retailer's site.

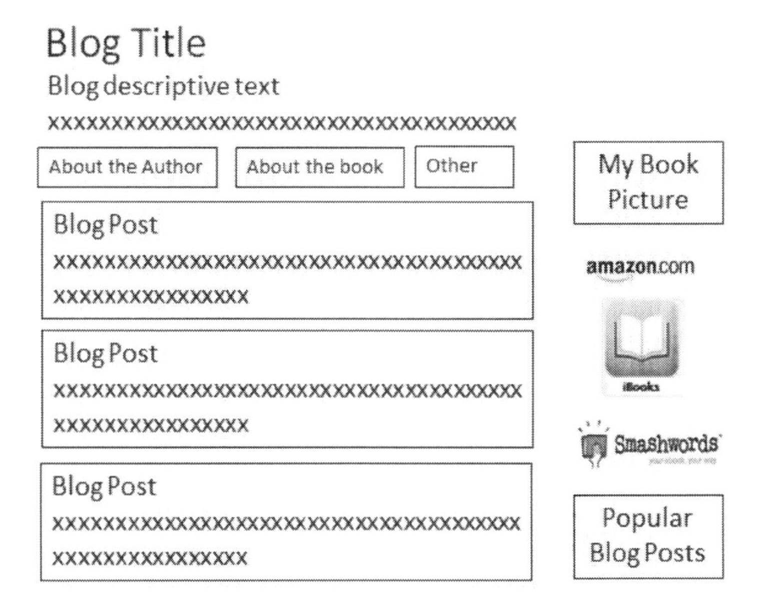

Figure 9 – Blog Layout

Once you make the pitch in your blog post, the reader is likely to click to the Amazon Kindle, Barnes & Noble Nook, Amazon paperback or the Smashwords link. This is the blog visitor's behavior you want to encourage. The blog reader quickly glances from left to right and then top to bottom, the only thing you want the reader to be attracted to is your book retailer's site.

Here is an example of a blog layout:

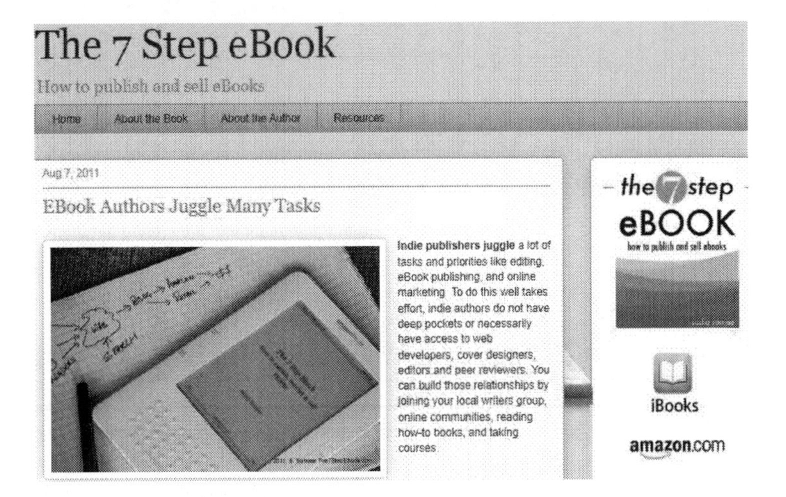

In the blog layout, the title is prominent with a short description under it, next your eye moves to the right showcasing your book in prime space. The book must be easily identifiable with purchase information under the image. If readers want to know more about the book or the author, they can click on the top menu.

The one-click rule

Minimize the number of clicks the buyer needs to make to purchase your book.

1. One-click to your bookstore, make it easy
2. Make the blog headlines standout
3. Keep your style consistent

Simple ways to attract buyers to your blog:

1. Share content that people want to know based on your reader profile developed in Step 2.
2. Post topics on a regular basis, at least once a week
3. Keep your topics short (250 words) and interesting

The 5 Point eBook launch

In Step 3, you built your platform with a blog, Facebook and Twitter and in Step 4; you published your book to Amazon.com, Barnes & Noble, Apple iBooks, Google Books, Sony, Chapters/Indigo, Smashwords and others. Ensure your reseller sites have been spellchecked, have the correct information and keywords before launching. Now comes the exciting part to announce your book and launch your campaign.

1. **On your blog**, post a notice announcing your book. Use the title, subtitle, description, benefits and keywords developed in step 2. Have a thumbnail picture of your book cover and links to all the sites such as Amazon.com that sell your book. Make the links very specific to land on your book page on the retailer sites.

2. **On Twitter,** tweet about your book and provide a link to your blog post announcing the book. Add a hash tag (#) to get the attention of potential customers. For example, if your book is about birding include "#birding" in your tweet. This hash tag word will show up in Twitter searches.

3. **Do the same** post on Facebook, LinkedIn and other social networking sites and link back to your blog post.

4. **Send a note** to friends and family announcing your book with your book announcement blog link. Respect people's privacy by placing the email addresses in the "BCC" field and not the "TO" field. Ask people to share this information with others. Add a signature on your email, as you are now a published author. The email should contain a link to your blog, which in turn has information about your book and where to purchase it. Note that your blog link in your email signature is a general link to your blog, while your book announcement link is to a specific post announcing the book.

5. **Develop and send** a well-written press release using a free press release services such as prweb.com.

STEP 6: MONITOR AND OPTIMIZE

Get into a routine of spending at least 30 minutes a day reviewing and responding to comments on your blog, Facebook and Twitter. Follow people, re-tweet and answer your messages. Keep present online with subjects developed in Step 2 to build your readership.

Daily social media activity

1. **Check Twitter messages** and review tweets from readers, publishers, magazines and reviewers. Tweet or re-tweet once a day. (5 minutes)

2. **Review your Google** Alerts and check news related to your book. Create a blog post acknowledging this and link back. (15 minutes)
3. **Check Facebook activity** and respond to readers, fans or post something related to the content developed in the Step 2, the marketing plan. Check your wall posts for new discussions. (5 minutes)
4. **If you have** a LinkedIn account, check industry related LinkedIn activity and stay active by responding on online forums and join relevant groups. (5 minutes)

Weekly social media activity

1. **Develop and post** articles of value on other blogs without selling your book. Participate in other blogs
2. **Provide online book** reviews on sites such as Amazon.com, Goodreads.com and Barnes & Noble
3. **Review Google Alerts**, if you have not set these alerts do it now (see Step 2.) Google alerts tap in the buzz about your eBook and similar books

Monitor your blog

Blogger "Stats" monitor where your blog visitors are from, identify posts resonating with your readers, assist to analyze trends, and continuously helps you improve your blog reader's experience

Go to your blog, sign on, and then click on the tab called "Stats." This tab will provide you with valuable insights about your visitors. The example below shows posts ranked by popularity; "Beaver Dinner Time" is the most popular with 11 page views for the week followed by 5 page views for "Chicks Huddle in the Grass." This is useful information to see which posts resonate with your blog visitors and which ones you should be focusing on in the future.

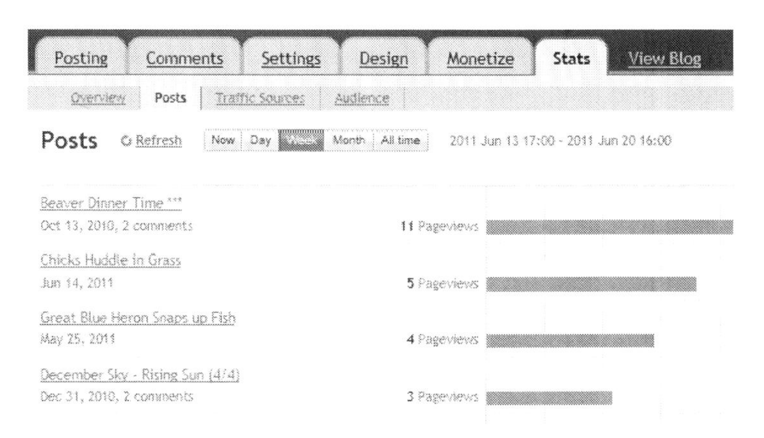

The Stats tab provides other intelligence such as countries your visitors came from (audience tab) and referring websites (traffic sources tab.) The world map display is

useful as it shows where your visitors are coming from. Darker shades indicate a higher density of visitors. In the map below, Canada has most visitors followed by the United States.

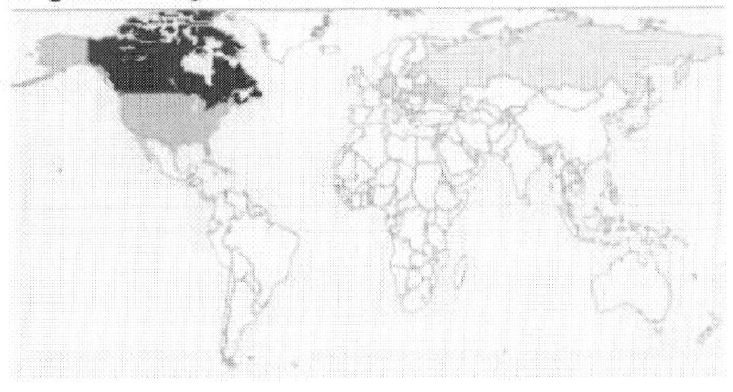

Expand on topics that have more views. Identify what worked on the blog posts. Was it the blog title, subject or content? With this information, you can focus on content that may be specific to a region or a topic. Expand on the topics that work for your readers. Experiment further and see what resonates with your visitors.

STEP 7: EXTEND YOUR SALES

The techniques and tools presented in Steps 1 through 6 are all you need for your book publishing and marketing platform. It is important that you use your blog, Facebook, Twitter, Amazon book page and Smashwords author page effectively before starting on Step 7. If you have limited time or are still getting the hang of these tools, then defer this step. This step builds on your platform by introducing video marketing, social bookmarking, and guest blogging, participating in online portals, and paid Facebook and Google advertising campaigns. You may apply all or part of these ideas in your online marketing strategy.

Video promotion

Promotional web videos are an exciting internet-marketing tool to create awareness about your book and draw people to your blog site. Like traditional TV commercials, these videos will promote your book to your target online customers. Producing a promotional video does not have to be complex or expensive. It can be created with some basic planning and storyboarding. Your video should be an entertaining infomercial that will attract your customers to your site. Promote your video on the hosting sites such as YouTube, Animoto and SlideShare. There is no reason why you cannot have the same video on multiple video hosting sites as each site will attract a different audience.

Storyboard

Before you start, visualize the video you want to create. Sketch out 5 to 10 frames and script out the story. In each frame, draw basic sketches and stick figures. Gather some images you want to include, perhaps your book cover, text from the book, and photos. Write some text to display on top of images to improve the message. Create an introductory slide with a title and a closing slide that reinforces the message. Keep your video under a minute with no more than 10 slides and leave the viewer with no more than 3 key messages. The message can be about the book in a short sentence and visual and where to buy the book.

Assemble your images, videos, scanned sketches and slides into a sequence using a video editing program such as Windows Movie Maker, Movie Editor on the Mac or any other movie maker program that came with your video camera. If you prefer creating slides, use PowerPoint or Open Office.

Create a YouTube account for your online video channel:

http://www.youtube.com/create_account

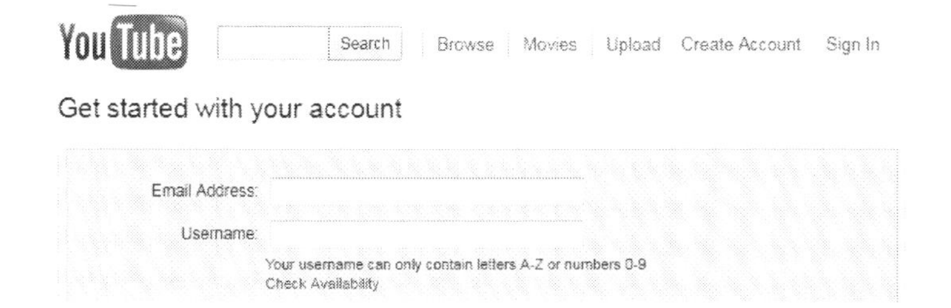

After you have filled in the YouTube account information, you will be permitted to upload your video on your YouTube channel.

Link and promote

Now that you have created and uploaded your video on YouTube, link your video on your blog and promote it by sending out a Facebook and Twitter update as described in Step 3. Write a brief description about your video on your blog and share the link by pasting it on your blog post.

YouTube has a large audience that you can leverage by adding keywords to your video and YouTube channel. Use the marketing information developed in Step 2 to fill out the Channel Tags. These keywords or tags will help YouTube direct viewers to your video channel. Since the YouTube audience is different from your blog, Amazon, Smashwords, and Facebook audience, your market expands even further. Each marketing channel adds value by creating awareness for you as an author and your book(s.)

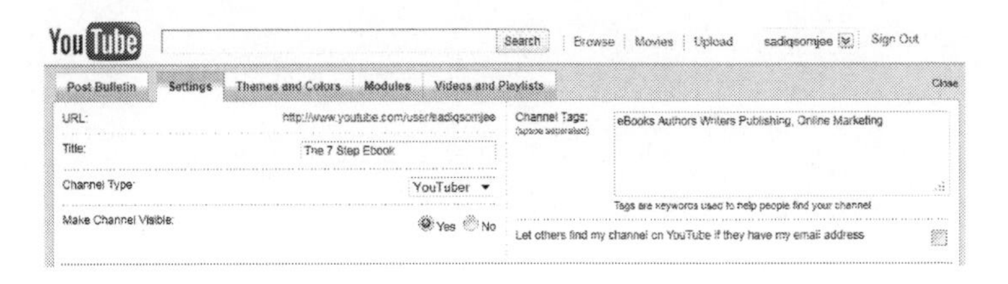

Google AdWords

Implement AdWords once you have built your platform and have an idea about the visitors to your blog. Before using Google AdWords, make sure you have exploited your own network on social media and email.

Google AdWords help you market and reach millions of customers for your book. You can spend as little or as much as you want on advertising. Google AdWords lets you reach a targeted audience back to your web or blog site. According to Google, 8 out of 10 Americans view AdWords each month.

AdWords provides information on how ads are performing; this allows you to tweak your ads dynamically to reach the most likely buyers of your eBook.

Before you unleash your credit card, think about your ad campaign. Suppose your book is about dog training:

1. Where is my audience and where is my book most likely to sell – Australia, USA and Canada or Global
2. Who is my audience – Dog owners, dog stores, dog trainers, and veterinarians
3. Google AdWords budget and pricing.

4. Read Google's documentation on:

   http://www.google.com/ads

Be sure to watch the online video "Getting Started with Google AdWords" on this Google link.

Facebook Ads

Facebook Ads target customers based on the information Facebook has about its 750 million members. The ads appear in the right-hand column of the readers Facebook pages. This is powerful way to reach Facebook members outside your network.

As a Facebook member, you can create Facebook Ads and target your ads based on location, age, keyword and other criteria. Try out Facebook's ads to see how many visitors land on your blog by using the Bloggers "Stats" feature. Estimate how many blog visitors turn into buyers by comparing sales before the ad campaign and after the ad campaign. Start with a small amount ($25) initially; Facebook will automatically stop your campaign if you exceed the amount authorized.

Facebook provides great reports on the ad performance and visitor demographics. On one test campaign, I discovered that 41% of the responders were 18 to 24 year old females and 20% of the same age group were males. 50% came from Great Britain, 32% from the US and 18% from Canada. This was incredibly useful information as the web pages and videos needed to be modified to keep this young demographic on the site longer. In addition, with Google Analytics, I could tell how long the web visitors stayed on a particular page, which told me which web pages worked well for them. Try these tools out and you will gradually learn how they work and discover more about your customers.

Design your ad with your book title and select keywords. When a viewer clicks on the ad, it will direct the viewer to online bookstore. The online store should have all the information required for the reader to make the decision to purchase your book. Keep in mind the one-click rule by minimizing the number of clicks and distractions to get to your online bookstore. The ad is your reader hook to get them to the purchase decision.

A word of caution about online advertising, it is complex and can get expensive, but it does give you an understanding of your reader demographic. If you are not inclined to bother with online advertising, stay with the Smashwords affiliate program. For 11% of the net sales your eBook will get great exposure.

Additional social bookmarks

When you create your blog (Step 3), Blogger automatically places a link to social bookmarks under each post.

These social bookmark buttons let visitors share your blog posts on their social networks. You can add other popular sites by signing on to your blog. Go into design, select a gadget such as "sociable", and drag it under your book link. Do not duplicate the bookmarks already provided by Blogger, for example, select:

Socializing on the web

Look for opportunities to contribute on other blogs by contacting the blog owner. Guest blogging increases exposure for your blog and book, it is another way to gain more exposure and generate traffic from a different audience. It helps improve your reputation as an author and provides a link back to your blog. View guest blogging as long-term opportunity to build online relationships and credibility.

Summary

Extending your market by creating promotional videos, participating on other blogs and advertising with Facebook and Google will provide your books significant exposure for free or for a small fee. Understanding your readers and designing your ads with the right keywords will return the most value.

SUMMARY

This book started with the big picture and explained how disruptive technologies such as eReaders, eBooks, online publishing, social networking and free online tools create opportunities for authors. Self-publishing with eBooks has leveled the playing field allowing indie authors access to the same markets that traditional publishers have dominated.

Building an online platform is necessary to market and sell your work. As you get to connect with groups on social media, you will discover groups and associations that will help promote your work.

We covered social networking tools, their benefits, why authors should use these tools and how the social networking tools like Twitter, Facebook and blogs all work together. In Step 2, you built a marketing template that you applied in the building, launching and optimizing of your platform.

Simple online tools were used to build an effective online sales and marketing platform. We walked through how to get your book published on an eReader with biggest share of the eBook market, the Amazon Kindle. Next, publishing on other platforms such as iPad, Barnes & Noble Nook, Google's Android, and the Kobo was described using Smashwords.

The book launch campaign demonstrated how to apply the marketing plan and platform created in the previous steps. The targeted Twitter, Facebook and Blogger posts in concert with an understanding of how search engines work provide an effective campaign to publicize your book.

With your eBook sales platform built and your book published, ways to monitor, optimize and extend your sales was covered. This book provided you with both the foundational concepts and a practical publishing and marketing platform to build on.

Keep the eBook success triangle (Figure 3) in mind and start with a quality book, build a great marketing plan, blog content that is of interest to your readers and connect using social media. With this platform, your book is discoverable and available for purchase online.

The eBook world is an exciting time for authors, as you now have a way to keep in touch with your readers, publish and market your work in this evolving and emerging market.

###

Thank you for purchasing this book and best of luck with your publishing adventures. If you liked it, please let other authors new to eBook publishing know about the book by posting a review on Amazon.com, Smashwords or any other retail website.

ABOUT THE AUTHOR

Sadiq Somjee is a graduate of Computer Science and has been in the information technology industry for over 25 years building, developing and managing technology solutions. He started his career as a software developer and he has worked for startup companies, internet companies, and large corporate clients.

He continues to work with technical specialists, sales and marketing staff on technology solutions. Sadiq is a freelance project manager and technology consultant.

ABOUT THE 7 STEP EBOOK

Visit the blog for purchase information, new discussions and resources on eBook publishing and marketing.

Web Site - **http://www.the7stepeBook.com**

Blog - **http://the7stepeBook.blogspot.com**

The free offer secret words are "Just Do It"

Email the secret words to **GeoEdge@gmail.com** and receive a project plan template for your eBook project.

Your email will not be shared or otherwise distributed.

Made in the USA
Charleston, SC
26 January 2012